James Field Spalding

The world's unrest and its remedy

James Field Spalding

The world's unrest and its remedy

ISBN/EAN: 9783741186295

Manufactured in Europe, USA, Canada, Australia, Japa

Cover: Foto ©Thomas Meinert / pixelio.de

Manufactured and distributed by brebook publishing software (www.brebook.com)

James Field Spalding

The world's unrest and its remedy

THE WORLD'S UNREST

AND

ITS REMEDY

BY

JAMES FIELD SPALDING

NEW YORK
LONGMANS, GREEN, AND CO.
LONDON AND BOMBAY
1898

COPYRIGHT, 1898, BY
LONGMANS, GREEN, AND CO.

All rights reserved

TO
HIS EMINENCE

JAMES, CARDINAL GIBBONS
ARCHBISHOP OF BALTIMORE

THIS BOOK IS
BY HIS PERMISSION
MOST RESPECTFULLY DEDICATED

Introduction

THE following papers, most of which originally appeared in the columns of *The Sacred Heart Review*, are republished at the request of many readers who believe they will be helpful to non-Catholics inquiring into the way of God's truth.

The author of these papers knows something what the unrest so prevalent in the religious world of to-day really means. He speaks from experience, too, of the remedy. It was the *genuine authority* which the Catholic Church proves herself to possess, set forth by thinkers like St. Augustine among the ancients and Cardinal Newman among moderns, which made such strong appeal to him some years ago when first brought face to face with his own obligation to truth. And though after his submission to the Church there followed a grievous period of "storm and stress," the end reached is the test by which he claims he should fairly be judged. The Lord in His mercy would permit that end to be only this—the acceptance of the Catholic faith, and gave him peace only in the "certainty and reality" of that faith. It is in part as a grateful acknowledgment of His mercy that he sends out this *Apologia*, if it may be so called, as well as thus to add his atom of testimony to truth, and possibly to aid some who are still striving and struggling. For all such he prays that, however long they may be left to toss upon the waters of unrest, they may at last find the haven of peace.

By thinking people, however many complications may arise in their minds as they consider the great question, What and where is the genuine religion of Jesus Christ?—and there were never so many complications as to-day—more and more will it be found that but one organization in the world can satisfy, for but one conserves the essential idea of the Church, the Divine Institution, God's revelation speaking with His authority to men.

> "Wanderers! come home! obey the call!
> A Mother pleads, who ne'er let fall
> One grain of holy truth;

Introduction

<blockquote>
Warn you and win she shall and must,
For now she lifts her from the dust,
To reign as in her youth."
</blockquote>

The author desires to thank all those who have expressed a kindly interest in the publication of these papers, and among others particularly the Rev. Daniel E. Hudson, C.S.C., editor of *The Ave Maria;* the Rev. J. Havens Richards, S. J., President of Georgetown College; and His Eminence Cardinal Gibbons, for many years a personal friend, who cordially accepts the dedication of the book and wishes it God-speed upon its errand of love.

Concord, Mass., *May*, 1898.

Contents

	PAGE
INTRODUCTION	vii
I.—GENERAL OBSERVATIONS	1
II.—IS NATURAL RELIGION ENOUGH? DOES CHRISTIANITY MEAN THE CHURCH?	8
III.—VAGUE NOTIONS OF THE CHURCH	14
IV.—THE CHURCH VISIBLE AND INVISIBLE—THE BODY AND THE SOUL	23
V.—DEFINITENESS—AUTHORITY—CERTAINTY	31
VI.—THE CHURCH'S UNITY	37
VII.—THE CHURCH'S HOLINESS	48
VIII.—THE CHURCH AS CATHOLIC	59
IX.—THE CHURCH AS APOSTOLIC	67
X.—FURTHER POINTS OF DOCTRINE—THE POPE'S PRIMACY AND INFALLIBILITY	78
XI.—THE POPE'S PRIMACY AND INFALLIBILITY	88
XII.—THE REAL PRESENCE IN THE EUCHARIST—TRANSUBSTANTIATION	99
XIII.—THE SACRIFICE OF THE MASS	112
XIV.—THE PLACE OF THE BLESSED VIRGIN IN THE CATHOLIC SYSTEM	123
XV.—HOW THE CHURCH TREATS SIN	136
XVI.—A FEW WORDS MORE UPON AN IMPORTANT SUBJECT	145
XVII.—MERIT, AS THE CHURCH TEACHES IT	157
XVIII.—THE SAINTS, AND OUR RELATIONS TO THEM	170

		PAGE
XIX.—	Personal Obstacles—Those which Catholics Might Remove	184
XX.—	Personal Obstacles—Those for which Inquirers are Responsible	201
XXI.—	Scope of the Subject—Certainty and Reality only in the Catholic Religion—The Return to Christ	214
	Index	231

The World's Unrest and Its Remedy

I

GENERAL OBSERVATIONS

THE present unrest of the world is a fact which people everywhere are admitting, and upon which they are variously commenting. Some deplore, some exult, some have vague or distinct fears, some a strange hope; while many, themselves actors in this drama, are so taken up with their own sordid pursuits as to look with indifference upon the moving scene.

There has always been more or less of this unrest. History shows it on wide planes of action, in the movements of races and nations, in vast upheavals, in wars and revolutions; and none the less every peaceful advance of civilization has had in this element the very law of its life. Its source is the restless spirit of man;—he is not the product of some chance, nor of hard force or impersonal law; nor does his spirit in its surroundings merely represent the infinity of nature girt around by the environment of fate. He is a creature, made in the very image of God his Creator. He is made *for* Him—to find in Him his chief joy; and because he is continually, however blindly, reaching out towards this end, he is restless. The words of St. Augustine are the true explanation—"Thou madest us for Thyself, and our hearts are restless till they find rest in Thee."

But any human condition generally true may have particular causes for unusual manifestations. And so here. This is an age of science, of seeking the ground for everything and the method of its working, in nature or in man; and the fact that science has often gone beyond its sphere and tried to give laws where it had no domain only shows how active is its agency in its far-reaching attempts. It is an age of mechanical invention, the manifold results of which have often transformed whole industries and turned the energies of the masses into new channels or left them unoccupied. It is an age of material comfort; and never before were there so abundant opportunities for what is called enjoying life, for those who have the means. In religion it is widely an age of doubt. Seeing is believing; at least there is an aversion to believing without seeing, and the unseen, the supernatural, is not credited. And because in all these marks of our age there is nothing that can really satisfy men, they are restless, and must naturally grow more and more so.

One can hardly ask for manifestations of this unrest. Are they not plain, save to those who shut their eyes? The prevailing discontent of our time is evident enough—everywhere showing itself—nourished by sensational journalism, secular or religious (?), and by much of the fiction which is widely read, and fostered by demagogues and ranters of Church or state wherever they can get a hearing. Throughout the civilized world men are going to and fro as never before, and knowledge is increased, and with knowledge a keen unrest to know more. Everywhere, especially in the great cities, are seen the hurry and turmoil of men in the race for wealth. The state of society is nowhere calm. Society seems in transition, to be entering upon new and unknown developments. Capital and labor and their relations are the burning questions, and they are not adjusted and perhaps never will be. The power of money grows and wonderfully centralizes itself; and despite philanthropic or socialistic schemes, more and more one may find the very rich and the very poor. Yes, in its discontent the world is living very fast; no form of government seems able to give both liberty and security; social evolution seems but just saved from becoming social revolution. The words of a recent writer are strikingly pertinent—" In living memory the world has never been in such a condition of unrest as it is now; there have never been at one time so many risks of explosion, where mine communicated with mine."[1]

What is the purpose of all this unrest of the modern world? To a great extent men do not know what they want—only they are uneasy, excited; but so far as they do know, their purpose may be legitimate and to be respected. In part it is *progress*. Stagnation

[1] *Blackwood's Magazine*, April, 1898, p. 559.

is death; motion is life, growth. To better one's self or the world, physically, mentally, morally, is not only permitted but commanded, and that by divine law. Again, the unrest of life is always looking forward to the goal of *rest and peace.* Men are slaves to toil; but they hope it will not always be so. They are greedy for money or fame, which they hope some day to enjoy in quietness. And even their religious doubts and fears which now so disturb they hope will somehow be answered in the great future, and that their souls will be at peace.

How is this unrest to be treated? Is there any power to help it?—to calm and guide the world, impatient for progress, looking for peace? Christ's religion is the great power to help man. It exalts him to the true end of his being, in God. Its message is the message of the Son of Man, who is also the Son of God. God was always in His world; but emphatically since the coming of our Lord. He is the beneficent healer of the souls of men. By Him alone this rightful aim of unrest can be directed, this fever of unrest be quieted. Christ's religion, faithfully observed, would answer all questions and meet all difficulties, individual, social, political—and would guide men through all rational progress to perfect peace. But how? In their individualism, or indifferentism—to accept or reject, as every one feels? No; there can be no ground of hope on any such basis as that. The religion which Jesus Christ founded—new, yet an expansion and adaptation of the old—is an organism, and life flows from Him, the Head, to all the members. It makes known a society, with laws and officers to govern and guide, with divine helps in worship and sacraments. This society is world-wide in its intended reach; and as it is meant for all men, to meet their deepest needs, so it has claims upon all, and to it all who would enjoy its privileges must belong.

His Church, then, is the embodiment of His religion. Therein He stands and pleads—"Come unto Me, all ye that labor and are heavy laden, and I will give you rest." Many heed; but why not more? Many accept a part of His teaching, but reject what they please. Why is not the religion of the one, holy, Catholic, apostolic Church of Jesus

Christ the panacea for the world's unrest, bearing sway over the hearts of all who so sorely need? What are some of the obstacles which hinder men from coming? These questions demand careful answer.

II

IS NATURAL RELIGION ENOUGH? DOES CHRISTIANITY MEAN THE CHURCH?

IN considering the problem of the world's unrest and its remedy, we are brought face to face with the various obstacles which hinder men from accepting the Catholic religion. Of some of these we propose to speak briefly in this series of papers; hoping that sincere, well-weighed, moderate, and charitable words may, by God's blessing, be helpful to one or another in this strife of life, in which we are all, whether we will or not, responsibly engaged.

All such obstacles may be accounted for by the weakness and baseness of human nature itself, and by the observed imperfections of Christianity as a human system. Men are too weak or too wilful to take God's way out of their trouble; often, too, they misunderstand and exaggerate the inconsistencies and contradictions—perhaps the scandals and enormities

—which have all along accompanied the workings of Christianity.

What are some of the manifestations of this spirit of rejection? For one thing, we see multitudes all about us going to the extreme of objection, and bent upon having nothing to do with Christ's religion. That so many of these are young men, educated young men, whose bringing up would warrant nothing of this sort, is all the more sad, and a bitter comment upon the power of the spirit of the age, and the apparent inability of Christianity, as actually seen and practised, to reach it. Young or old, what do they say—these wholesale objectors? That *natural religion is enough for them.* They would not call themselves deniers of God—indeed, they have a kind of belief in Him; but they say they see no need of any religion beyond that of nature—the natural reason, the untaught conscience. This they claim is simple and practical and teaches them how to live from day to day; and if they can do their duty in the various relations of life, personal, domestic, civil—if they can be true and pure and kind and self-sacrificing, that is all they can attend to, and all that God asks of them.

Now there is much that is correct in this way of putting the matter; and the harm is chiefly in its inference, so false and defective—an inference of completeness. Nature or the natural order—its truth and virtues—is not in contradiction with the supernatural order. Natural religion is good so far as it goes; and Christianity, the perfection of revealed religion, builds upon it. And why not? A man is a man before he is a Christian; but what we claim is that the perfection of manhood can be reached only through Christianity.

Natural religion is not enough; and to infer that the natural virtues are all God requires of us is mere assertion. Natural religion never really satisfied the heart of man; and every such system has ended in mere theory, like Comte's boasted religion of humanity, or has gone to pieces in practical failures too manifest to require denial. Natural religion can not meet man's needs nor his aspirations. The needs are from the fact of his sinfulness; and here there is no sufficient account of sin. The aspirations pre-suppose sin forgiven and its power more and more conquered; and then they reach out for a perfection, in this life and the life beyond, of which natural religion knows nothing. Christianity is the only religion which provides for all this. How can the doubters of its worth account for the simple fact of Christianity in the world? If the natural is enough, why the supernatural? The only alternative is to deny the supernatural; and to such straits are they driven, though thus they do violence to the very laws of their being.

To be truly reasonable, then, in view of all their condition, men must go on from natural to some kind of revealed religion. For present consideration we may throw out of our thought all other systems, and come to Christianity. Let us suppose this in some way accepted. But what shades of assent among those who call themselves Christians! And it is not for us to judge how sincerely men are living up to their light and responding to the grace of God, but to thank Him that that grace is everywhere, to pray that the light may shine clearer and stronger and that more may see and follow it. Cardinal Newman said he was a Catholic because he was a Christian; and this conclusion seems plain enough; but how long a time was he not so!—and for all outside the visible fold we must wait God's time of leading, and always be charitable in our judgments.

Every difficulty in the way of those who remain without while professing to be Christ's disciples it would seem must inevitably centre around the idea of a church. The lowest plane supposable is that of those who *do not recognise any church at all.* Jesus Christ they own as their divine Saviour; love for Him, we question not, is their inspiring motive; and they claim to be devoted followers because of this personal love; but they have a morbid dread of what they call ecclesiasticism, they are most suspicious of anything like dogma, and would make the whole of practical Christianity consist in the precepts of the Sermon on the Mount.

But really, these simple, primitive Christians, as they call themselves, appear to have the least possible ground for their position. Did not Christ speak plainly of His Church? Did He not establish that Church upon the rock, Peter, and promise that the gates of hell should not prevail against it? Can this solemn act and promise of His be explained away without weakening all His other acts and promises? Did He not command those who were in controversy to " tell it to the Church," and did He not say that whoever would not hear the Church should be regarded as a heathen or a publican? Further, supposing the rest of the New Testament to be consistent with the Gospels, and apostles to be carrying out the injunctions of their Master, how can any Christian fail to read the divine institution of the Church of Christ in Gospels, Acts, and Epistles?

Yes, we can not see that it admits of question that the Church is bound up with the very existence of Christianity, and by the express will of the divine Founder—that if there is no Church there is no Christianity. We need not meet formally the difficulties of those who dwell so much upon their personal love for Jesus Christ. Why should not that personal love be just as strong in those who believe in the Church—who find in her worship and sacraments its surest safeguard and its deepest response?

III

VAGUE NOTIONS OF THE CHURCH

NON-CATHOLIC Christendom professes to make its appeal to the Bible; and although in our day the Bible is not the acknowledged authority it once was—is, alas! being much despised or ignored—the influence of its teachings remains, and is seen, however perverted, in the hold which its great doctrines or precepts or institutions have upon the community at large, even those most easy in their living or free in their thinking. And what institution of Holy Scripture is more fundamental or pervading than that of the Church? So, while there are very many, as we have already noted, who are trying to live in entire independence of God's institution, a church of some sort is still generally recognized as representative of Christianity, and most Christian people regard themselves as its members.

But in that Protestant world of which we

Vague Notions of the Church

are now speaking how vague are most of the notions of the Church—and increasingly so, by the very law of development, as Protestantism runs its course! It may be hard, indeed, for many of our separated brethren to own it; but let us all admit *what is true*, whether in fact or in tendency.

There are scores of sects—Baptists and Methodists and Congregationalists and many more—but no one of them, as a body, ventures to call itself, in its formularies, the one true Church of Christ, or if there is an occasional exception to this statement, as, *e.g.*, with the Irvingites, who style themselves " the Catholic, Apostolic Church," or the high-church party among Episcopalians, who speak of that denomination as " the Church," —such assumption only provokes a smile from their fellow Christians. And not only is there this general lack of definite, authoritative claim in most of these sectarian bodies—and so their very concession that there are other churches is an admission that they are all only sects, and perhaps a glorying in it—but the same principle seems to be bearing fruit very widely nowadays, in the spoken or written teachings of the Protestant ministry, or in the common sentiment of their people. There is nothing strange about this, nor do we so present it. It is the natural growth of the root-principle of Protestantism—this vagueness of notion growing more vague continually, as to what the Church is, what is its origin or authority, if it have any, what its mission, what it is doing in the world or proposes to do.

As instances of what we refer to;—it is well known that Congregationalists, as one of their writers has recently declared, "do not believe that the form which Christianity took at first *was intended to be permanent;*" and one of their most eminent divines[1] not long ago said he even doubted "whether Christ appointed the two principal sacraments to remain in the Church for all time." In the platform which this sect has lately put forth as a basis for unity, "the great mission of the Church of Christ" is declared to be "to preach his Gospel to the world"—which is only a half truth at best; and when there is coupled with this that other article of their platform— "Liberty of conscience in the interpretation

[1] Rev. Dr. Lyman Abbott.

Vague Notions of the Church

of the Scriptures and in the administration of the Church"—there is clearly manifest that very uncertainty of Protestantism which must always come from the principle of private judgment. On the other hand, this sect sharply criticizes the Lambeth articles of the Episcopalians, and calls their historic episcopate " a vague phrase interpreted by some to mean one thing, and by others to mean something very different "; and who shall say there is not truth in the charge? One is reminded of Dean Stanley, who loved to assert that " the historical church of England was built upon compromise, and her history had been one of compromise." This, to him, was its real comprehensiveness. A minister of this most " comprehensive" communion boldly proclaimed, a while ago, that in the Church of the future the sacramental would have less and less force, and the ethical would be the chief thing; and so urged his people to study Tolstoi and Ibsen to learn the realism of life. Verily, what is the Church?—and what is its meaning? Well—as another instance—a late well-known prelate used to teach that " every human being, in virtue of his birth, is a potential member of the Christian Church"; which is either a harmless truism or a position from which many would go on to unsafe conclusions. His thought seems to be in a line with the opinion of the English broad-churchman, Dean Freemantle, who has written a book—*The World the Subject of Redemption*—to show that the Church is as wide as the world, and that the Christian ministry is to disappear.

It is not surprising that with such notions as these—and we have only given a few specimens—it should be considered the right thing, in so many quarters, to have "no standard of belief," but "a perfectly unfettered Christian liberty"; that the merit of a recent book upon *The Christ of To-day* should be said to be that it represents "not the Christ of dogma, but a personality that expresses what most feel that Christ ought to be"; that henceforth it must be "a bond spiritual, not dogmatic" which is to unite Christians; and that it should be claimed that "insistence on creeds, symbols, and forms of church government has destroyed unity."

If these are indications of the state of opinion among the leaders of Protestant thought, what shall be said of the people themselves? Their notions, too, inevitably correspond. Such a current of teaching cannot be without its effect. There are exceptions; but we believe we are safe in affirming that the greater part of non-Catholics all about us have *no definite idea of the Church as an organisation*, nor consider that there is anything in doctrine, or sacrament, or worship to hold them together. The Church has become, in their minds, the most shadowy conglomeration of all who call themselves by the name of Christian. Many of the churches are coming to be little more than clubs for the cultivation of the social element, or nurseries for " Christian Endeavor Societies," so-called; while the claims of divine worship are supposed to be met by the people coming together on Sundays to be moved by sensational preaching or to enjoy artistic music.

It can not be claimed that there is no sincere religion in the midst of all these manifestations. Far be it from us to say there are not as sincere non-Catholic Christians as Catholic Christians. But the religiously-minded ones among them we believe are living more and more a life of religious individualism. And their churches can give them little relief. There was pathos in the ringing words of a distinguished delegate[1] to the last Episcopal General Convention (1895), even if on a somewhat different line of interpretation from what he meant: "I tell you that the fountains of the great deep of American Christianity are breaking up. Who can look abroad upon the phenomena of the social and religious life of our day, and doubt it? Why is it that *we do not know what to call ourselves?* Why is it that we sit here and discuss day after day *what we are, and why we are?* You find the same uncertainty, the same unrest, everywhere. The fountains of the great deep are broken up." Yes, you find, plain enough, that same "uncertainty and unrest" everywhere in Christendom outside the Catholic Church. You do not find it within that Church, either theoretically or practically. Even in that particular Protestant communion which draws nearer than any other to the Catholic Church in many points of doctrine and worship, what definiteness of view is

[1] Rev. Dr. W. R. Huntington.

there? Does the broad-churchman want any definite idea of the Church? Can the high-churchman or the ritualist have any? What or where is the Church, as they picture it? Is there any such organization in existence? It is hardly worth while to argue that the Church, on the "branch theory," is only an ideal creation of the mind.

So one and all among our non-Catholic brethren are feeling, unmistakably enough, the influence of these vague notions of the Church. Some are cherishing them, and fancying they see in them the bright light of spiritual liberty, or at least the harbinger of the dawn of Christian unity. Others really oppose them, while they confusedly try to live near God in spite of them. More than one honest non-Catholic have we heard say in these trying times, "Well, I believe in God, and I try to serve Him." Perhaps in their discontent they resolutely withhold allegiance from any particular form of religion, and devote themselves to morality alone; for—they say—is not conduct three-fourths of life? Many take refuge in the theory of an invisible Church. They feel there is little to help them in such vague notions of a visible Church as are rife. They think they might about as well have no Church.

Whether cherishing or opposing, all are really kept back from the one true Church of Christ by these vague fancies. That is the fact that is so lamentable. In this sad unrest of the modern world they can find no peace. There is but one way of peace—God's way—the way of His truth.

IV

THE CHURCH VISIBLE AND INVISIBLE—THE BODY AND THE SOUL

THE theory of an invisible Church beneath which many are taking refuge in these days of unrest is one that must be fairly met and disposed of. We suppose it is the honest conviction of most of our non-Catholic brethren, so far as they have any conviction upon the subject. At all events, from their traditions, the Protestant denominations in general would cling to this theory, excepting the Presbyterians and a certain section of the Episcopalians. And while there is a sense in which the theory is true—as we shall explain—in the way in which it is generally held it is the most evident untruth, a contradiction of terms.

For what does it mean? That an institution which Christ established for the salvation of the world has no marks by which it can be seen and known. This in itself would be most strange; it might be called *prima facie* impossible. We pass by, as possibly figurative, the reference to His disciples as "the light of the world," "a city set on a hill." But certain positive appointments of His can have no significance, if the Church is only invisible. Apostles and an apostolic ministry are for naught. Sacraments are of no force. These ordinances appear to tell of an institution before the eyes of men: if they do not, they tell of nothing; there is no such institution as the Church of Christ.

Truly it is "a despairing idea," as it has been well called. When did it originate? It is often said that the germs of all heresies may be found in the first few ages; and yet it will be hardly contradicted that, until the Protestant Reformation, three hundred years ago, there was never a serious claim that the Church of Christ was not in the plainest sense *visible*. That idea first took definite shape with Luther, when he rebelled against the Church and led that dreadful schism which has brought such confusion upon the world and from which Christianity has found it so hard to recover. He, in his infatuation, must present some radically new notion to the minds of men; though we know from history how reluctantly even he was driven to this fancy, and how inconsistently he maintained it. The Church is *not at all the visible organization*—Luther taught—so full of sin and corruption; it is an invisible ideal, known only to God. And so, instead of persisting in reform within, of which no one denies there was then need enough, he enticed himself and his followers into the great sin of revolution and rebellion. We need say nothing of the many personal questions which might arise at this point, nor of what may be true as to Luther's own life and character; we simply affirm that the theory of an invisible Church—as against the visible—ostensibly set up for greater purity of living, would not naturally accomplish that end, and has not accomplished it. As even a distinguished Anglican writer, with whom we are happy to agree, puts it [1]—" all stress laid upon the invisible Church tends to lower the demands of holiness. . . . It is a visible Church . . . which calls out the fruits of

[1] In *Lux Mundi*, p. 377.

faith into active energy"; — and whatever purer morality there has been or is in the Protestant world, is either only natural, not Christian morality, or is from the working of Catholic principles, which more or less pervade Christendom, and which have their source in God's own institution, the visible Church.

Indeed the idea of a visible Church of some sort has all along partially mingled with that of an invisible one. But in our own day, as perhaps never before, many in their unrest are driven from even this resource. They are caring less and less for such "visible" churches as their sectarian bodies present to them. We would have all such see that the purely "invisible" Church of their fancy can have no sanctions, no authority, is only a phantom. We would bring them to accept the one visible Church of Scripture and of all history.

With this they may and must accept, as all Catholic theology teaches, the great truth of the invisible Church. For there is a sense, as was observed at the outset, in which this is true. The Church of Christ is both visible and invisible. As that eminent Catholic theologian, Dr. Schanz, says: "The kingdom of

God will be like Christ Himself; its strength divine and invisible, its main purpose and means spiritual; but itself, like the God-man, must take its place and position amidst a world of sense."[1] There is the *body* of the Church and there is the *soul* of the Church; and a clear understanding of these two existences and the relation between them we are persuaded would help many inquirers for the truth out of the difficulties which so trouble them as they look upon the confusing scene which Christendom presents no less to-day than in all the past.

What is the soul of the Church, and what the body? The sure possession of spiritual gifts must mark the soul; and external confession of faith and use of the sacraments the body.[2] To use the language of a recent writer, Father Hunter, S. J.—"They only belong to the soul of the Church who, if the question were now to be settled, would be found to have secured to themselves the fruits of the Redemption; . . . in other words, the just and the just alone constitute the soul

---

[1] *Christian Apology*, vol. iii., p. 51.
[2] *Id.*, p. 300.

of the Church." Again: "In these three elements, baptism, profession of belief, and communion with those who have authority in the Church, especially by reception of the sacraments administered by them, we have all that is required to constitute any one a member of the body of the Church."[1]

Accordingly the soul of the Church must be ever invisible. God alone knoweth who are the just—who are His. The visible Church contains both good and bad, and in all degrees of goodness and badness. This is why the Church exists—to make the bad good, and the good better. And there are even those who are utterly bad; vilest hypocrites who will never change. But as man cannot certainly know who these are, they remain—the cockle growing with the wheat till the harvest. And even till the moment of death God teaches us to have hope for the worst.

So there are many, always, who belong to the body of the Church who are not of its soul. But further, many also belong to the soul who are not of the body. Here the divine charity shines forth. In the words

[1] *Dogmatic Theology*, vol. i., pp. 263, 266.

of Dr. Schanz once more: "The Catholic Church, while maintaining her claim to be the one saving Church, admits a distinction between the objective doctrine and its subjective application, and recognizes an internal connection and necessary relation between the visible and invisible Church. All in the Catholic Church will not be infallibly saved, nor will all outside it be irretrievably lost." . . . "What are called *bona fide* heretics must in all justice and fairness be morally considered members of the one true visible Catholic Church, though they are not visibly in her communion." . . . "Nor does God's mercy stop here. The heathen are not left without all hope and comfort. Little as the actual life led by the heathen gives ground for sanguine hopes, still they always retain their natural power of knowing God, and the voice of conscience proclaiming His eternal law is ever resounding within them."[1]

Surely all this is broad enough for any reasonable man. In the one body alone are all the spiritual gifts in perfection; that body

[1] *Ut sup.*, pp. 293, 298, 301.

" visible in association," as Father Hunter so well says—" with a bond of union knowable by the senses, and of such magnitude as to attract attention to itself." With that body all who have sufficient knowledge and opportunity are bound to connect themselves. God alone can be the judge of the limits of ability and obligation. He alone knows who are living up to the light that is given them, and who are wilfully rejecting His call in remaining without. All who are wise will seek earnestly to be numbered in the invisible Church, the true soul, by membership in the visible body, faithfully using the gifts of grace therein bestowed.

V

DEFINITENESS—AUTHORITY—CERTAINTY

THERE is genuine satisfaction, as every one may know, in a definite, positive idea upon any subject. Upon that most vital and all-engrossing subject, religion, it is as necessary as it is satisfying to have such ideas. God does not mean His children to be continually groping in mists and shadows of uncertain speculation, but to have them walk in the clear light of a reasonable faith.

Accordingly, in the treatment of the subject before us, it is a satisfaction to have done with the various vague and contradictory notions of the Church, and emphatically with the wildest notion of all—that of a purely invisible Church—so unreliable and aggravating. Let us suppose these fancies all given up. Thus the way is open for accepting the one definite revelation of the visible Church of Christ; and so, for any who are really disturbed and inquiring to find direction for their impatient energies, relief for their unrest.

It may be well to mention at this point that it is by no means the purpose of these papers to enter upon elaborate proof of Catholic doctrine. There is manifest good in presenting such proof anew from time to time, not only in books, but in the columns of religious monthlies and weeklies which come before the people, and which serve a missionary end as well as strengthen the faith of those who already believe. The present aim, however, is somewhat different. Touching upon this or that point relating to Catholic position, claim or proof of claim, perhaps occasionally stating more fully the Catholic teaching as to certain doctrines or usages, we would seek chiefly to bring before our readers the reasonableness of that teaching, which we shall rather assume than prove to be the full, normal revelation of Christianity.

Catholic truth, then, presents, for one thing, just that *reasonable definiteness* required in a religious system meant to meet the widest needs of the souls of men. It tells of the being and character of God, of the character, duty, and destiny of man in no uncertain terms. It tells of the Church, her ministry, worship, and sacraments, her precepts, usages, and discipline in a way not to be misunderstood. Not that the Catholic system always draws hard and fast lines for believing or living. It does not; and herein is shown the divine wisdom which is its source. What is of the faith (*de fide*) is clearly laid down, to be believed. What is not of the faith—and very much belongs under this head—is left to the freedom of individual opinion and expression. A great many mistakes arise among non-Catholics concerning Catholic belief and practice from supposing that to be authoritative which is not—but which is only the opinion or teaching of some individual theologian, or parish priest, or layman; or perhaps the permitted custom of some country or people. So, too, you may sometimes hear a loud cry of wonder, perhaps with a note of malignity, at some adaptation to the age on the part of the Church—which professes to be always the same. But the Church never professed to be rigid and unyielding in everything. She can change, when necessary, in matters which are changeable.

Hers is the present and all the past, the living voice and the verdict of antiquity. In matters of faith she always has been and always must be the same, fixed and unchangeable; whatever may seem to be the variation, the latest dogma is no contradiction to the earliest; both are only legitimate unfoldings of the original deposit of the faith committed to the apostles.

In matters essential Catholic teaching can be definite on the strongest possible ground—because it speaks with divine authority. What necessary dignity and power are thus given to the true conception of the Church! Why will men continue talking of the Church, of membership in the Church, of ways of governing the Church, of the ministry and worship of the Church, when they mean merely some arrangement of human device? All human arrangements can be only vague and indefinite at best. Divine authority alone can give definiteness; and wherever this definiteness is found, naturally it is taken as tending to prove divine authority; while indefiniteness is quite conclusive proof that such authority is wanting. Who can imagine the divine institution, the true Church of Christ, giving an uncertain note to the world as to its nature or functions, or even whether it exists at all?—not knowing the source of its authority or wherein that authority is seated?—not quietly taking for granted its own infallibility? In the honest answer to such simple inquiries as these all who will may find for themselves a safe criterion by which to know God's institution in the world, what it is and where it is.

Allusion has just been made to infallibility. The word is a bugbear to many non-Catholics —they are afraid of it, as of some flaunting "rag of Popery"; a misapplied term with many, who mistakenly imagine they accept it. The idea, in its true significance, as applied to the Church, is eminently reasonable. If Jesus Christ is God—and this we assume—if there is any meaning in His promises of being with His Church to the end of time, and of sending the Holy Spirit to guide into all the truth, if His Church thus guided is now, since His departure, taking His place in the world, her voice must have the same certainty as His voice. When the Church speaks, He speaks; and as there could be no mistake in His utterance, there can be none in hers.

The difficulty in men's minds at this point must be either that they do not accept His speaking as infallible, or else that they do not understand when or how His Church speaks. The difficulty thus covers the case both of those who reject the idea of the Church's infallibility, and of those who think they accept it but remain outside. These last cannot really accept what they think they do, so long as they refuse obedience to the lawful, divine authority of the Church. Would that any such who chance to see these words might be led by God's Spirit to revise their convictions and submit to His infallible guidance in His infallible Church. Thus would they be consistent, and would know the worth of definiteness speaking with a certainty which can spring only from divine authority. Thus would there come, as can not come otherwise, a certainty to their own faith. For how can any be certain of a revelation which is not really infallible?

VI

THE CHURCH'S UNITY

THE Nicene Creed declares the Catholic belief to be in "One, Holy, Catholic, and Apostolic Church." These four adjectives designate what are commonly called the four notes of the Church. All these qualities are important, yes, essential; they are not to be regarded as merely interesting, or appropriate, or expedient, but as describing an institution which, though human, is also divine, the prerogatives of which bespeak a divine necessity. These are God's own marks put upon His Church; found in Holy Scripture, read in the creeds, and corroborated by history. Singly and together they distinguish the true, visible Church of Christ from all other Christian bodies—a claim of distinction which can be made with the utmost charity.

Unity is oneness. The Church's unity means that there is one Church and only one, and that in all essential points there is a necessary degree of concord among its members.

We shall not delay to show that our Lord would naturally establish but one Church, and that this was what He did establish. Any other mode of organization would have been absurd; nor did that divine charity which would gather together into one all the nations of the earth do anything to foster the divisions of selfishness and ambition. Further, the conditions of the case are not satisfied by a merely spiritual unity. Those who claim that originally there were a number of independent local bodies bound together by this inner tie, and say this was all that unity meant and still means, while they apparently escape from the difficulty of divided Christendom, both contradict the stupendous fact of Catholic unity existing without question for fifteen hundred years, and salve over the trouble of to-day's divisions with an ideal sentimentalism. The Church's unity is both spiritual and organic; the "unity of the Spirit"—the Holy Spirit of God—pervading the body of Christ—Christ's own organization among men and of men. As the Church is visible—and we need not further argue this—it demands a visible unity; and any other kind of unity, under guise of however high terms, substitutes human feeling for divine truth, and must continue to fail of the Lord's very purpose in appointing unity, which was—to be a witness to the world of the divine power of Christianity. What kind of a witness is a merely spiritual unity? What witness that which covers, or assumes to cover, radical differences of belief, government, worship, and sacraments?

These are the essential points wherein there must be a necessary degree of concord. These define the Church's visible unity. In going on to speak of them, it will not lessen the force of our considerations to own that this unity is one which permits and even encourages much variety—which often exists, too, in the midst of much discord and strife. The Church is made for man, not man for the Church; and God's institution adapts itself to his nature, weak and imperfect as it is, and means to mould it gradually to the divine perfection, by strictness in a few great principles, by a wise discipline combining severity and gentleness, and by a wide freedom under

authority; "not the freedom"—says one—
"to roam and blunder *ad libitum*, but the
freedom of truth, the freedom of children,
wherewith the Son of God has made us free
in His kingdom of truth."

The Church's unity is a unity of *faith*, of
belief. This may be called its leading characteristic. All else is meant to guard this, its
chief quality. The faith is the body of doctrine divinely revealed; and as all this truth
of God is at the foundation of Christ's religion,
which is meant to be for our highest blessedness throughout eternity, it follows that the
acceptance of this revelation—full and unquestioning belief of it—is a matter of first importance. It is of the region of faith, not of
that of opinion, that we are now speaking;
and as to matters of faith there can be no uncertainty, no division, no contradiction, doubt,
or denial. God's truth in Christianity must
not be imperiled, must not be weakened or explained away. For the sake of each individual Christian, for the sake of the Church and
the world Christ died to redeem, there must
be unity of faith, unity in the faith. As Dr.
Schanz writes: "It was the Church, equipped

The Church's Unity

with creed, authority, and sacraments, that established unity in faith and discipline, and saved Christendom from being splintered into countless Christian and unchristian sects."[1] And with her constant power of definition in every age the Church has subsequently spoken once and again, by the sure guidance of the Holy Spirit teaching her the full meaning of the divine truth once revealed. These doctrinal definitions are not new revelations, but the official declaration of the exact meaning of the old; and always there has been preserved the same unity of faith. Heresies and schisms have arisen all along; but these have not destroyed, but rather have proved, unity in the Catholic Church.

Those outside the Church who do not possess this unity may sometimes ridicule it as impossible—say it is only a thing of words; or if inclined to regard it as a reality may wonder how it can be secured. As to the impossibility, the fact speaks for itself; all the cavils of sectarians and freethinkers and deniers can not shake the fact that the entire Catholic Church believes the doctrines, *e.g.*, of the In-

[1] *Christian Apology*, vol. iii., p. 180.

carnation, of the Real Presence of Christ in the Blessed Sacrament, of the Blessed Virgin's Immaculate Conception, or of the Pope's Supremacy and Infallibility. How unity of faith can be secured may perhaps be learned by looking at a second point of Catholic unity.

That is a unity of *government*, and of *discipline*. Not only does this statement mean that there is essentially one kind of government in the Catholic Church, but to point out that the leading idea of that government is in a centre of unity. The bishops throughout the world, succeeding to the office of Christ's apostles, constitute the Church's governing as well as its teaching power; but as St. Peter, one of those apostles, received from our Lord a primacy of honor and jurisdiction among them, so the Catholic principle of rule makes it necessary that the Pope, the successor of St. Peter, should be at the head of the hierarchy. There is much involved in this visible headship of the visible Church which we shall speak of further on in these papers. The point we wish now to bring before the reader is that thus there is gained a centre of unity which becomes the surest safeguard for unity of faith. What the Church really believes is not made a matter of question, one saying one thing, another another. There is an interpreter of revelation, whose voice infallibly speaks, when necessary, as the voice of the Lord Himself on one hand, and as the voice of His infallible Church on the other.

This unity of government and discipline naturally covers a wide reach of events and affairs large and small; and practically there might be a widely varying usage in many particulars from one age to another, or in different lands under different phases of civilization. Such is the fact. Discipline more strict in one time or country, *e.g.*, in reference to penance or fasting, is relaxed in another; and still the principle of unity is kept. It is real government, real discipline, for both priest and people. If sometimes there seems to be too great rigidity, it can only be said that strictness is often necessary in all right government, but that tyranny was never the divine ordering for the Church, and that wherever it has existed it has been a human abuse and not a divine sanction.

The Church's unity of *worship* and *sacra-*

ments is perhaps more impressive than either of the other features of unity of which we have spoken. All the sacraments are unfailing bonds of unity. Clearly distinguishing the one Church—as we claim they do—they also help to make it one. We are baptized by one Spirit into one Body; and even where irregular, baptism, if validly administered, is into the one, holy, Catholic Church, and there can be no wish to escape from this charitable provision. And so of the other sacraments. All of them are held, administered, and received throughout the world with a harmony of spirit and of act which bears clear witness. All of them, and emphatically the Holy Eucharist, bind the hearts of the faithful in the one communion of saints to the sacred heart of the one Lord.

As for unity of worship, reference needs to be made only to the worship of the Mass. The dignity of the Holy Sacrifice preserved in unity through the medium of the unchanging ancient language—the words and action of the Mass, whether with or without music and incense and rich ceremonial, always the same in every land and time—presents to eye and ear and heart a teaching of unity which has no equal. And yet this very unity of worship exists with widest variety; for worshipers, as all Catholics know, have abundant privilege. The mystic sacrifice is being offered for them and for all the faithful, living and departed. They take part in this sacrifice by their devout recognition of what is being done for them—and the ritual is a great help to both ignorant and educated—while their sincere intention is consistent with varied offering up of the heart to God in prayers and praises which spring from individual sorrows or joys or needs. There is not the uniting of *voice* in this worship—an element of outward unity which many converts miss for a time; but while there is no inherent reason why this should not be encouraged, the very liberty which now exists would be thereby endangered, as the broadness of Catholic freedom came to be exchanged for an uncatholic rigidity of form expressing itself in a volume of sound!

The practical bearings of this subject of unity upon that of the world's unrest are not far to seek. And yet upon no subject is there more flagrant misconception. Everywhere thinking people are lamenting the divisions among Christians—the hundreds of sects and beliefs and ministries and kinds of worship. The deep feeling upon the matter is a good sign—that the Christian community is more than ever appreciating how disastrous these divisions are to Christian life and growth, and especially to the spread of Christ's kingdom among men. But all the agitation and discussion, the plaints and prayers, among non-Catholics proceed upon the assumption that Christian unity is lost. Somehow, they don't know how, it is to be restored; and the schemes are as many as are the fancies of men. But unity has not been lost. It is a gift bound up with the Church's very existence. If there is no longer Catholic unity, there is no longer anywhere the visible Church. But no! to-day, as ever, there is the one faith, accepted and followed; to-day, as much as when St. Irenæus[1] told of the Church of Rome to which every other church must resort because of its superior authority, or as when St. Cyprian[2] told of the beginning being

---

[1] See his treatise "Against Heresies," bk. iii., ch. 3, sec. 2.
[2] In "The Unity of the Church," secs. 4, 5.

made from unity (in St. Peter), "that the Church may be set before us as one,"—there exists that centre of unity in the Apostolic See. Unity, thank God, is not lost. Men have departed from unity; and so they are living, more or less culpably, in separation. What is lost is the true conception of the nature of the unity of the Church.[1] For healing the divisions of Christendom Catholic prayer and effort may best be directed to restoring that conception. Thousands of our separated brethren, perhaps the great majority of them, may still resent any such method as the overture of ignorance and arrogant conceit. Very well. Yet Catholic unity, strong and firm as in the beginning, in spite of all heresies and schisms and departures—this is Catholic belief and always has been. And we do not fear for the final result. To call back the wandering to the home of unity—to do so with humility—is the work of charity. God's Spirit works, and, breathing where He wills, He moves the hearts of men.

[1] We wish all might read the fair paper of Wilfrid Ward upon "The Rigidity of Rome" in *The Nineteenth Century* for November, 1895.

VII

THE CHURCH'S HOLINESS

It is hard to gage the relative importance of the different marks of the Church, for, as has been said, all four are to be regarded as necessary. In a weighty sense unity is at the foundation; holiness, catholicity, and apostolicity are built upon that—find their full meaning and right interpretation only as they grow out of that divine principle. Yet how essential is holiness! Not only does every Christian conscience admit this necessity, but owns, besides, that if the Church is not holy, the world may reasonably enough say there is no Church, no Christianity, no religion; though in any case it is reasonable to ask, calmly, on the other hand, what men are looking for in insisting upon holiness, and to make no false and weak issues.

Holiness is the distinctive character of God. Both as regards absolute perfection and as regards absolute moral worth this word best describes Him. What we claim for the Church primarily is, that, as God's institution, divinely endowed, divinely guided, it possesses necessarily this attribute of holiness. The Church is the mystical body of Christ; and we as correctly think or speak of the holy Church as we do of the holy Lord, the Church's Head. All this can not here be argued; it is presumed to be admitted by all who believe in the Godhead of Jesus Christ, and who have any true notions of His Church. In a derived sense, also, whatever relates to God, whatever is brought into particular connection with Him, is holy as well. Why, then, are not the declared institutions of the Church—thus under the promised guidance of the Holy Ghost—its sacraments, its Scriptures and traditions, its apostolic ministry, its places of worship, its utterances of preaching, prayer or praise—why are not all these holy? Indeed they are; and so acknowledged, with greater or less strictness, by the common sentiment of Christian people. Accordingly, we shall not now further treat this portion of the subject, interesting as it is.

But what is the design of these holy ordinances which tell of the holy God? Plainly, to make men holy, like God, that so they may better honor Him and be fitted for that holy joy and fellowship which He promises. Here is the practical meaning of the Church's holiness—that its members are holy. Does the Catholic Church carry out this design in its members? is the vital question. This holiness, it must be remembered, is a moral quality; it reaches to character, to thought and motive as well as to conduct. Owing to this very nature its existence cannot always be surely determined. Moreover, there are degrees of holiness. Great numbers, too, outside the visible communion of the Church possess holiness, and numbers within that communion have it not. All these are points of more or less difficulty which must be touched upon, even if they can not be fully discussed within the limits of a few pages.

While it is true that the Church's holiness is a visible mark, it can not always, like unity, be demonstrative. Who can distinguish sincerity from hypocrisy? Only God Who reads the heart and knows who are His. Christian virtue, too, is not naturally forth-putting. A demonstrative holiness would run great risk of being a contradiction, even an imposture. Faith, hope, charity, humility, purity, truthfulness—the Christian graces in general—do not ostentatiously parade themselves. Even on these general grounds how widespread may be that holiness of which the world takes no account! Stirring events, marked opportunities may indeed visit any life, and develop heroism, which becomes public example and shines henceforth on the page of history; but the virtues of thousands upon thousands of the faithful shine only before the eye of God. The vast majority of holy lives, the world over, are being lived in the midst of the ordinary routine of care and duty, in circumstances of daily trial which are known well enough to those who suffer them but which attract little attention. In this connection particular reference may be made to the genuine holiness of multitudes of the poor who have the faith. Can this be doubted, has it ever been fairly questioned, quiet and unobtrusive as it is and hidden from public gaze? Yet all classes, rich and poor, high and low, learned and ignorant, can have this gift, can show this character. They are expected to have it and show it, and it can not be denied that they do. The Church is not an abstraction, nor its holiness only a theory. In spite of all obscurity and uncertainty—and we have meant to give full weight to these conditions—the Church throughout all the world, with its thousands of holy prelates and priests, its thousands of holy men and women devoted to the religious life, its millions of faithful people, displays holiness transfused, like light, throughout its membership. Various types of piety and virtue are seen among Catholics, differing according to race and country or other environment, here one grace prominent, there another, but the reality of all is its own witness and is beyond contradiction. The good tree must bear good fruit.

The fact of varying grades of holiness only goes to strengthen our general statement. The ideal, of the Church "glorious, without spot or wrinkle or any such thing," is not yet attained. That is foretold by the apostle as the Church's destiny. The question now is, is there actual progress towards it? That there is may be clearly seen even from the regular, consistent growth always going on in a multitude of individual lives. Our appeal here must be to experience, and we are sure this would make good our claim.

The lower grades of Christian holiness may bear close resemblance to mere natural virtues —indeed, how often do these virtues in such as profess nothing higher for themselves put to shame the goodness of those who possess divine faith!—but everywhere and in all ages there have been vast numbers who have gone beyond this, who, by the grace of God, "bestowed and nourished through the ministry of the Church," have lived the truly supernatural life. These are verily the good fruit of the Church's teaching, and their virtues are an undeniable witness to the world. These, indeed, are saints—holy ones, and if they persevere to the end they will form jewels in the crown of rejoicing of the heavenly King at the last day. And are there not those who, even in this life, have soared to yet grander heights than any we have mentioned? who, through self-sacrifice, patient suffering of trials, voluntary labors and humiliations and chastisements for Christ's sake, living in the world or apart from the world, have risen above it to that closer nearness to God which has made them worthy the distinctive title—*saints?* Yes, there have been many such. Some of them known to us through the Church's honor, some unknown, all in that shining company now reigning with Christ in heaven, now our blessed intercessors, are the highest proof of the Church's holiness.

What if this gift of holiness be also found outside the Church's visible communion? If there is any truth in what was said recently in these papers about the body and the soul of the Church, such a supposition is not in the least strange. It would be strange, indeed, if it were not so; for that would imply that God's grace, which is everywhere striving with human souls to bring them to the truth, is *not* given in response to sincere desire and according as we live up to the light we have. Only they who are weak in Catholic principle or ignorant of Catholic truth can presume that genuine holiness is not found outside the one true fold. Further, such a statement is consistent with the other, that holiness is an exclusive mark of the Catholic Church. The doctrine of the Church's body and soul reconciles the two positions. "I see no reason," says one of our wisest and most learned theologians, "why we may not admit that the supernatural virtues of faith, hope, and charity subsist in a great number of sincere and religious persons, separated from the external communion of the Church, but virtually and spiritually united with it. However, no matter how many members the sects may have who are holy, their holiness is not derived from any sect, but from the Catholic Church."[1] So our rejoicing in the fruit of grace thus found means no encouragement to the evil of wilful separation. We are not, indeed, judges of individuals. To his own master each one standeth or falleth; but "heresy and rebellion," as Father Hewit declares, "are in themselves only noxious and demoralizing, and tend to the destruction of Christianity."

Again, numbers of those within the visible Church are not holy, but unholy, wicked and godless. And this, it must be owned, is a

[1] Very Rev. A. F. Hewit, D.D., in *Am. Cath. Quart. Rev.*, October, 1896, p. 724.

far more serious matter. Not only are there grades of holiness, but grades of unholiness, in the visible Church. Saints and sinners are found side by side, like the good and bad fishes in the parable. But make the wickedness as bad as we may, it does not, it can not, touch the principle of the Church's holiness. For the Church has always taught a pure and holy doctrine; and those who obey that doctrine become holy. The unholiness was all predicted by the great Head of the Church; and hard as it may be to accept as a fact, we can partially understand how in wisdom it has all been permitted. It has always been so; the evil has borne fruit, too, in all classes; popes and bishops and priests as well as people have been bad. Yet right in the midst of the worst have been the best; and the darkest epochs of the Church have been distinguished by great numbers of saints.

As to the relative holiness of Catholics and Protestants in any period of the Church's history, controversy appears to be worse than useless. There is always temptation to make too little of our own sins and too much of those of our neighbor. Catholics have had to

The Church's Holiness

bear a great deal of base calumny. They will probably have to bear a great deal more. The best way to meet it is to go on speaking the truth in love and striving to make lives consistent with professions. The coarse, low maligning sometimes heard on either side—to say nothing of its being so unchristian—is beneath decent people. Let Catholics look to their own sins—clear their own skirts. That is all they are responsible for. There is nobody among us but knows what a stumbling-block in the way of people, otherwise favorably disposed, perhaps earnestly seeking the truth, is "the example of bad and careless Catholics." And the Catholic Church, to her honor be it said, is by God's grace doing every day and in every quarter of the world the noblest work in trying to restore and save these very ones, so unworthy, so sinful. She does not give up this heroic labor; she does not rest day or night. Indeed, it would not be amiss to hold that " her one great mark of holiness—a mark altogether peculiar to herself—may be found in her ministry of reconciliation, her sacrament of penance, in her attitude towards sinners and unquestionable influence over them. To those in darkness she brings light; to the erring, rest; to the despairing, hope and peace."[1]

Is there not here, we may well ask, a portion of the remedy for the world's unrest?

[1] Schanz's *Christian Apology*, iii., p. 346.

VIII

THE CHURCH AS CATHOLIC

This term Catholic is the most common of all the titles applied to the Church. It is so familiar that we are apt to forget what it means, and what a grand and glorious heritage it proclaims. The idea is that of universality. The thought which at once suggests itself is the close connection between Catholicity and unity. The one Church must have been intended to be universal, and the nearer it comes to being actually so the more is the world at large impressed by its unity.

The Church is called Catholic, then, as representing that universality which was the aim of its Founder. If the word itself is not found in holy Scripture, the idea is there, in the commission of our Lord to the apostles—" Go ye into all the world, and preach the Gospel to every creature,"—" Go teach all nations."

Naturally the early Christians, as they saw the Church spreading from city to city and from country to country, would begin to think of the destiny divinely foretold and promised; and before very many years one and another of the Fathers were speaking of " the Catholic Church," or " the Catholic Church spread all over the world." The earliest recorded instance is in one of the epistles of St. Ignatius, about the close of the first century, and from this time on the expression was increasingly coming into use.

Although the expectations of the apostles and some of the early Fathers proved, as we know, to be literally too sanguine—as were their ideas in reference to the speedy second coming of Christ and the general resurrection—the title remained, to be more and more justified in its divine ordering by the progress of events in the world's history. Heresies and schisms sprang up and multiplied. The Catholic Church was by this very title distinguished from all the sects; and this became an aspect of its significance which was thus clearly defined, and it is one which must never be forgotten as we consider it. This was the " title of honor

The Church as Catholic

which all men agreed to give her, which furnished a more simple direction than epithets of abuse to aid the busy and the ignorant in finding her, . . . one which the sects could neither claim for themselves, nor hinder being enjoyed by its rightful owner; though, since it was the characteristic designation of the Church in the Creed, it seemed to surrender the whole controversy between the two parties engaged in it."[1] St. Augustine, in the fourth century, says he is held in the Catholic Church "by the consent of peoples and nations, . . . and lastly by the very title of Catholic, which this Church alone has so retained, that if any stranger were to ask where to find the Catholic Church, not one of the sectaries would dare to point to his own chapel or house"; and a modern writer well points out that what St. Augustine here meant to express by the title was, "not an opinion but a fact; it indicated what was that body which was known to exist throughout the world."[2]

So it made no difference, a few years later,

---

[1] Newman's *Essay on Development*, etc., p. 254.
[2] R. I. Wilberforce's *Principles of Church Authority*, p. 86.

how numerous or how pure in morals were the Donatists, against whose schism he so strenuously contended; still he told them, "securus judicat orbis terrarum," etc., "the collective body—the universal Church—securely judges that those can not be good who separate themselves from this body in any part of the world." These were the words, it will be remembered by all familiar with Newman's *Apologia*, which kept ringing in his ears the knell of the Via Media of Anglicanism upon which he had been hitherto so depending.[1] And the same principle which applied in relation to the Donatists was even more strikingly illustrated during the two following centuries; for though Arianism and other heresies then so overwhelmed the Church in different countries that the title of Catholic seemed a misnomer, as a fact the title was kept, and history does not yield the slightest proof of any attempt to deprive the Church of it. Thus in the midst of all vicissitudes there would seem to have been preserved an identity of type which has marked God's institution in every land and in every age.

[1] *Apologia*, p. 116.

Looking again at the title in its primary signification, it is pertinent to ask,—what is the actual condition of things to-day? Is there a nearer approach to universality than in the past? As regards extent of domain there has been great advance, and this is continually going on. Through its compact organization the missionary zeal of the Church has spread the true faith far and wide into the different countries of the earth. As regards relative growth in numbers, it can only be said that out of the approximate population of the world, put at about 1,445 millions by careful authorities, some 450 millions—less than one-third—are reckoned as Christians, and of these not more than 240 millions—a generous estimate—are Catholics. Such a statement as this, at first, perhaps, startling, appears to leave little ground for complacency or idle boasting, certainly little for supineness of any sort. We do not mean to discourage; but it is always well to look facts in the face. There is every reason for labor and self-denial, every incentive for prayer and patient effort. Christianity in any form is far from possessing the earth; and, certainly, the Catholic Church is yet far from realizing its ideal of universality. "Catholic" is still in this sense a prophetical title, as Newman once spoke of it.

Yet each of the notes of the Church, while inherently a divine mark, is not to be taken by itself, as if there were no others. So Catholicity does not stand alone. The Catholic Church is also inherently, really, and progressively holy; the Holy Catholic Church is truly apostolic, and completely one. Even in its progressiveness a genuine visible quality, how wonderfully is Catholicity strengthened by unity! Look on this picture, then on that. The millions of non-Catholic Christians are divided into a thousand communions large and small, each clinging to its own phase of truth, or holding various separate truths, more or less distorted fragments of *the truth*. Even on merely human grounds is it likely that any or all these sundered sects will ever attain Catholicity? The millions of Catholics the world over, of many races and tongues and tempers, are one in the great essentials of faith, discipline, worship, and sacraments; bound together, in all their variety, by a divine unity, never lost, never broken. They do not believe in sects, nor can they trace anything more than a human system in so-called national churches. They obey their priests and bishops in all duties rightly enjoined; they yield loyal reverence and submission to the Holy Father at Rome, not as an "alien power," a "foreign despot"—as he has been falsely styled from ignorance or malice—but as the divinely appointed visible head of the visible Church on earth. Is it not these millions, and not the others, who are in the way of attaining the Catholic ideal?

We do not forget that there is a sense in which Catholicity is to be spoken of as a finished quality, an absolute possession. Nor do we mean now any reference to the mere title used to distinguish the Church from the sects. Catholicity is broadness, comprehensiveness, grandness of vision, noble generosity of thought and action. In all the variations of this use of the term, so far as they can be applied to religion, the quality belongs supremely to the Catholic system. "A local religion is not from God," whatever Godlike traits it may show, or whatever divine truths it may preach. The Church is Catholic "because she brings a universal remedy for a universal disease."[1] Striving by every rational means to heal souls of that disease—severe against the sin, merciful to the sinner—the Catholic religion beyond all others adapts itself to the varying needs of all classes of men. Holding and insisting upon a few great principles, it allows beyond these a wide liberty. It is the broadest religion on earth that is worthy the name of a religion. Rightly viewed, generously and intelligently accepted, and implicitly followed, it would bring the world out of its slough of pessimism into the wide plain of cheerfulness and hope; out of its fever of wretched unrest into the calm enjoyment of divine powers and gifts, the exercise of which would not be bounded by the limits of place or time but by the universe of God and the eternal hereafter.

[1] Newman.

IX

THE CHURCH AS APOSTOLIC

It is not strange that the Church should take one of its names from those men who, under Jesus Christ, were its founders. And this name, apostolic, indicates a mark as essential as either of the others. Indeed, apostolicity has been correctly called the attribute which "by itself furnishes a complete guarantee that the Church was instituted by Jesus Christ"; and wherever this decisive test fails, there the true Church does not exist.

But there is a great deal of loose talk and looser thinking nowadays as to what is meant by the Church's being apostolic, and whether there is anything binding in what the word describes. Some, calling themselves Christians, are of such falsely progressive liberalism as to repudiate all connection with what is ancient. The apostolic is to them the obsolete, the effete, the "creed outworn." The undisguised contempt which such people express for anything relating to the twelve poor fishermen, certainly anything authoritative, is the counterpart of their joy in what they call the new faith, the modern Christianity. Most non-Catholics, it is to be hoped, do not go so far as this. They still revere the name of the apostles, and to a greater or less degree their office and their labors. They sincerely believe themselves possessed of the apostolic spirit; they insist that their organizations be so known; some of them cling tenaciously to what they call an apostolic succession.

In view of all this state of things it is well to try to explain a little what is meant by genuine apostolicity as a further mark of the one, holy, Catholic Church. We can not expect to win over any who scout the very idea, nor to move any whose self-satisfaction in their now imperfect conceptions is supreme; but perhaps some who are tossed by the present unrest of the religious world may at least be set thinking whether here, in apostolicity, is not an added element of stability, and may resolve to reach out, with whatever self-sacrifice, for a faith which is consistent, harmonious, and complete. This they will find nowhere but in the Catholic Church.

The Church is apostolic, then, primarily in possessing an apostolic ministry, by which is meant one continuously handed down from the apostles. The divine Lord must have intended this continuity when He gave those chosen men their commission. For He not only laid upon them the various duties of their ministry and promised the Holy Spirit's power and guidance, but He added, "and behold I am with you all days even to the consummation of the world." They were to live in their successors; and Scripture and history plainly show that this has been from the first the interpretation of the divine intention. So the apostles proceeded to ordain others who should succeed to the necessary privileges and functions of their office. And so, ever since, the Church has had bishops, who constitute the highest rank in its hierarchy, and whose particular, exclusive function is the power of ordaining to this apostolic ministry made up of bishops, priests, and lower ministers. Further, as one of the original twelve, St. Peter, was given the first place of honor and jurisdiction among them, and is rightly called prince of apostles, so his successor in that see of Rome becomes prince of bishops. The papacy is the legitimate conclusion from the primacy of St. Peter. The Pope as the head of the hierarchy is an element essential to the apostolic ministry of the Church. It is impossible to have a genuine apostolic succession without this element.

A brief digression at this point may not be out of place. It would seem as if the severe shock which some of our mistaken brethren have lately received in the decision of the Holy Father against the validity of their orders might be the means of leading them now to see, even without regard to the Papal decision, and all the more with its added weight, how defective is that fancied succession upon which they are so fondly leaning. What can be the worth of that which has the name of descending from apostles, if it does not recognize a necessary feature of apostolic rule and claims independence of the Apostolic See? When Anglicans broke from the centre of unity at the Reformation, they lost the succession; and lost it just as truly, in the Catholic sense of the word, whether their orders remained valid or not.

Again, the Church is apostolic, in teaching and holding the apostolic doctrine. The teaching power of the Church is in the bishops, with the Pope at their head; and if these are true successors of apostles, why should they not teach apostolic doctrine? In fact, if this could not be guaranteed, of what use would be an apostolic ministry? But it is guaranteed by the Lord's promise to be with His Church till the end of the world, and by His express words to the apostles, that the Holy Spirit should teach them all things and guide them into all truth. Revelation ends with them; and the bishops, their successors, guard the deposit of apostolic doctrine, bearing intelligent witness to what they have received, —explaining, defending, yes, "developing it according to the needs of each succeeding age." Thus the Church acts as the divine interpreter of all revelation, and this whether contained in apostolic writings or in apostolic traditions. The Church also teaches in dogmatic definitions and in the decrees of councils, and all this teaching is and must be apostolic.

Furthermore, the whole body of the Church, clergy and laity, receives and holds fast this apostolic doctrine. Clearly it would be of no avail to have it taught, if it were not believed. But as the early Christians, we read, "persevered in the apostles' doctrine," so it has been ever since. What is taught with divine authority is *de fide*, and is bound to be accepted by the faithful. Heresies of many kinds have arisen, sometimes drawing after them individual bishops, or even sections of bishops—as with Arianism and Nestorianism—but whether such heresies have subsided or continue their baleful influence, or whatever new ones may arise, the Church as a whole has continued and will always continue apostolic, faithful in its allegiance to the truth of God revealed to apostles and handed down by them and their successors from age to age.

Two principles may be plainly seen to be bound up with the Church's apostolicity. One is its infallibility. The Church can not err in its definite, authoritative teaching. The apostles were infallible teachers, each and all thus inspired by the Holy Ghost. Through them the divine Lord would guide the faithful,

The Church as Apostolic

and would bring all men to the knowledge of the truth, that they might be saved. Can it be, then, that He mocks men by authorizing or permitting error to be presented in this teaching? And if it be said that each individual bishop is not infallible,—neither, it may be replied, is that necessary. Infallibility is " invested in the Church as a whole, as one organic body," and is attached to the apostolic office and the apostolic power; and it manifests itself, by the divine assistance (to use a theological term), in him who holds the fullness of jurisdiction in the Apostolic See and in the bishops acting in union with him.[1]

The other principle to which we refer is that of indefectibility. The Church, because apostolic, can never fail. The apostles live in their successors and will always live. They will continue to teach and govern, and the great body of the faithful will continue to believe and obey. This is the method which the Head of the Church takes to carry out His promise that the gates of hell shall not prevail against it. He builds the Church upon the

---

[1] See Schanz's *Christian Apology*, iii., pp. 228, 262, 264. Father Hunter's *Dogmatic Theology*, iii., pp. 396, 397.

rock of His chosen apostle, and in connection with him upon all the rest of the apostolate and episcopate to the end of time.

To call the Church apostolic because it continually manifests the apostolic spirit would be a most natural sequence from what has been already said. Nor would such a claim be any unmeaning inference—stating but a vague generality. The genuine apostolic spirit can flow only from the genuine apostolate; from the office and the men who still represent Christ's original institution, from the Church with just such a ministry, so teaching and so believing. That spirit, too, will inevitably distinguish the apostolic Church; it can not be otherwise; but when those who have no apostolic ministry and succession, who exercise no such authoritative teaching nor require such believing, talk of their showing the apostolic spirit, with all charitable judgment we must maintain that they are making a false claim or that they use language very loosely.

What are some of the legitimate manifestations of this spirit?—it may be asked. Go back, for a moment, to the original apostles. They were men sent forth upon a most difficult and dangerous mission, yet one under the highest sanctions and looking to the grandest results. They went forth strong in the divine authority, cheered, comforted, supported by the divine Presence breathing a benediction upon them. The apostolic spirit then meant the union of many noble qualities of mind and heart—yes, if we take into account all that the Holy Spirit's guidance signifies, the highest possible gifts and powers. We are not to forget that they were men, however inspired and infallible; their teaching that of "living, intelligent witnesses," their office human as well as divine; and it is on the human as well as the divine side that we can honor and be thankful for their apostolic spirit—their zeal, their courage, their humility, their wisdom, their patience, their undying hope, their unbounded charity, their invincible perseverance.

Now it would be a truism to say that the apostolic Church shows and always has shown these same apostolic qualities; but what we affirm is, rather, that the one, holy, Catholic Church by these and such qualities continues to prove itself worthy the name apostolic. Instances need not here be mentioned; the record is upon the pages of history; in times of persecution, of pioneer effort, of far-reaching missionary enterprise, of social, civil, national danger, of needed wise legislation on any account, as well as in the continuous everyday life of the Church at large, these are the qualities which have not failed to shine forth. It is no idle boast which the Church thus makes. Whatever exceptions may be fairly adduced, let them be admitted; they but heighten the beauty and glory of the truth. Weakness and sin are done away, or transformed by God's grace into holiness and strength, and the human is perfected in the divine.

The Church as apostolic looks back to the dim past, reminds us of antiquity. But antiquity is not everything. Hers alone is also the continuity of teaching and worship and sacrament which binds the past with the present. She speaks with the voice of the living teacher. Together with the reverence and dignity of age she reveals the freshness and glow of perpetual youth. With the same divine qualities as hitherto—fired with the same zeal, the same courage, the same hope, the same charity—she must go on to possess the future. The promises of God are hers.[1]

[1] In this series of papers it is our purpose to take up next a brief consideration of a few other leading Catholic doctrines, with the hope of showing their reasonableness; that instead of being a sufficient obstacle to prevent men from accepting God's way of truth they are rather the best helps to individual spiritual growth and happiness and for remedying the world's unrest.

X

FURTHER POINTS OF DOCTRINE—THE POPE'S PRIMACY AND INFALLIBILITY

In brief review of the ground hitherto gone over, what we claim is that the religion of Jesus Christ is the sure remedy for the world's unrest, and that the Church of Christ is the living manifestation of this religion. Vague, uncertain notions of the Church, as we have shown, can not satisfy. There must be something definite and authoritative, an institution visible and with credentials proving its divine origin. To all who will open their eyes and use their reason this divine institution is plainly pointed out by the four marks which have been just considered. The Church has come down from Christ's own apostles essentially unchanged yet legitimately developed; it is Catholic in spirit and purpose and in its ever-widening growth; it is absolutely holy in its origin and ideals and progressively so in its membership; it is one in faith, discipline, worship, and sacraments.

Here we might fairly rest our case. But we are endeavoring to meet obstacles in the way of honest seekers for truth, not merely to present unanswerable claims. With this motive, some plain words upon certain further points of Catholic doctrine may be pertinent. Such a course seems desirable in view of the mistaken ideas which continue to oppress the minds of so many non-Catholics. In spite of the larger knowledge of our day which the Catholic spirit is doing so much to spread in various ways, in spite of the wide toleration which God's providence is overruling to the doing away of bigotry and the furtherance of candor all about us, there is still a vast amount of deep-seated prejudice among sincere Christian people who do not think and believe as we do. They may respect and even admire a great deal in the Catholic religion; but they could never—they say—make this religion their own,—could never accept it nor submit to it. This or that teaching is absurd, this or that destroys their freedom, and so on. Prejudice keeps them where they are, though they are by no means at rest. And so they will continue—disturbed, dissatisfied, without the approval of conscience, grievously uncertain whether they are pleasing God or doing good to their fellowmen. But who can estimate the power of such prejudice? How varied and how subtle is its working! All we need say is this: so far as it is the result of honest ignorance, it ought to be enlightened; so far as it springs from conceit and wilfulness, we must leave it with God, and only pray more earnestly than ever that the Holy Spirit would move all hearts to a willing obedience.

As already hinted, it is not intended in these papers to enter into formal, detailed proof of Catholic doctrine. That would often require a treatise rather than a page or two; and also, upon general grounds, such treatment may more properly be left to theologians among the clergy. It is our wish to state upon competent authority what the Catholic teaching is, and perhaps what it is not, and then to show the reasonableness of what is taught; that instead of being an obstacle to prevent men from accepting the Church, there is here the best reason why they should accept it; that this teaching offers the truest help to individual spiritual growth and happiness, and, if generally received and acted upon, would furnish the effectual remedy for the world's unrest.

The present topic—the Pope's primacy and infallibility—it is well to meet at the outset. Purposely we place it first. According to the Catholic faith the Pope is the visible head of the Church on earth. This is the central doctrine of the Church's organization, in a vital sense the keystone of the arch of all Catholic teaching. Here is the crucial point of distinction between Catholics and all non-Catholics, whether Greeks, Anglicans, or other Protestants. With good reason this position may receive first consideration.

Let us state a little more fully this matter of headship. The Pope, the bishop of Rome, we claim is the successor of St. Peter. Now it was this apostle alone whom Christ made the rock of His Church; to him alone He promised the keys of the kingdom of heaven; he alone was assured that his faith should not fail, and was bidden to strengthen his brethren; to him alone the good Shepherd solemnly entrusted the care of His lambs and His sheep —the entire flock. These plain grants, which have never been explained away, are amply enough to declare a headship, a primacy conferred upon him—no mere honorary primacy either (by which some Protestants own him *primus inter pares*), but one of authority and power, that is, of jurisdiction. Peter, according to all Catholic interpretation, was to take the place of Christ, that is, to become, in His absence, "the visible supreme shepherd, guide, ruler, and teacher of all Christians." It has been well said that if Christ did not mean to make Peter His vicar on earth, no words could have done it; and this headship, in Christ's place, we claim Scripture and all tradition show he exercised. But as the apostles were to live in their successors (which we have already shown), emphatically St. Peter; and the need of our Lord's bestowing upon him this primacy meant that it was not to die out with him. Indeed, to use the words of an eminent authority: " Peter's position and office and the existence of the Church are correlative. If he ceases to exist, the Church *ipso facto* collapses. Such is the direct, obvious and natural force of the Scripture passages."

Here, again, it is the Catholic claim that facts support theory and inference; that the voice of tradition, the testimony of the Fathers, the decrees of councils—all going to form the witness of history—tell of this primacy of the bishop of Rome, a gift and a power more and more manifest. It is not assumed that it stood forth in its fullness at first, " as a scheme minutely drawn out," but that it was " a living, intelligent force"—the breathing of the life-giving Spirit in the living body,—a power which " grew and developed, like everything else in the Church, with time and circumstances, its application becoming more extended and intense as the need arose."[1] The Pope, then, as St. Peter's successor, is the vicar, the vicegerent of Christ, the head of the hierarchy, the visible head of the Church, the rightful supreme teacher and ruler of all Christians. This is what Catholics mean by his primacy or supremacy.

The Pope's infallibility is but a chief function of his primacy. It necessarily marks his

[1] See Schanz's *Christian Apology*, iii., pp. 479-80; 495-96.

supreme power of teaching. It follows from
the infallibility of the Church, which, as we
were recently saying, is directly connected
with its apostolicity. The apostolic power, the
apostolic office, has always been infallible, by
the gift of the Holy Ghost; and the successor
of St. Peter, holding the fullness of jurisdiction, is divinely assisted to speak without
error. According to Catholic faith the appointed visible head of the infallible Church
must speak thus, with unerring certainty,
when he acts alone as Supreme Pontiff just
as truly as when he acts in connection with
the rest of the hierarchy. The authority is in
the head alone as well as in the head and
members combined. There is but one infallibility, as there is but one authority.

Because the dogma of Papal infallibility has
been but recently defined, it must not be
deemed a novelty in revelation, an addition
to the faith, as Protestants sometimes call it.
New definitions do not mean new revelations.
Non-Catholics do not seem to understand this.
Some of them, we fear, *will not*, when we note
how they stop their ears and cry out in holy
horror,—the Church of Rome is adding to the

faith! It is, indeed, out of the beaten track of thought of those who cling only to antiquity and disown the Church's present, living voice. But the Church can not add to the faith. The germ—the principle—of this doctrine is in Scripture, a part of the apostolic deposit of revelation concerning the primacy, and, like that, it grew and developed. Nor is there here, as Cardinal Manning has clearly shown,[1] any fair instance of the triumph of dogma over history. As matter of fact, history declares that the Popes always claimed the right of giving an infallible decision in questions of faith, and often acted upon this claim. By consistent development, then, and in accordance with a fixed law—that denial of truth calls out its vigorous defence and formal definition—the opposition to the Church's infallible authority from the time of the Reformation on for three centuries at length brought the definite statement of that authority to its full and final issue in the Vatican decree of 1870.[2] It

[1] In his *Religio Viatoris*, p. 78, etc.
[2] All this is very strongly and at the same time popularly brought out in Father Hecker's instructive book, *The Church and the Age*, p. 10, etc.

is a natural and logical conclusion. The Pope is at the climax of infallible authority, as he should be. In this, as in other respects, to borrow the happy expression of a recent writer, "if the bishops are the leaves of the Christian plant, the Pope is as certainly the flower."

But the Vatican definition is most carefully worded. It declares that "the Roman Pontiff, when he speaks *ex cathedra*, that is, when in discharge of the office of Pastor and Doctor of all Christians, by virtue of his supreme apostolic authority, he defines a doctrine regarding faith or morals to be held by the universal Church—by the divine assistance promised to him in blessed Peter, is possessed of that infallibility with which the divine Redeemer willed that His Church should be endowed for defining doctrine regarding faith or morals." It may be clearly seen from this language that the doctrine has its provisions and its limitations. The bare, unqualified statement that the Pope is infallible may give a very erroneous impression to any non-Catholic mind, and with the wilfully ignorant or the ill-disposed may pave the way for such base slanders as that of our teaching that the Pope can not sin, or even that the Pope is worshiped as God—slanders which are by no means unknown in our enlightened day!

How is the Pope infallible, and *when?* In our next paper we shall go on to answer this question by the aid of the Vatican definition, and shall then consider the reasonableness of the primacy and its attendant infallibility.

XI

THE POPE'S PRIMACY AND INFALLIBILITY

THE Vatican definition declares *how* the Pope is infallible and *when* he is infallible. His infallibility, for one thing, is the same as that of the Church; a power which originally spoke through the apostles, and was meant, as we have seen, to give an intelligent, human witness. The Pope is the final witness to the apostolic tradition. "No one maintains," says Dr. Schanz, "that the Pope can decide by a mere word of command, or that he can dispense with the ordinary means of evidence for tradition." Many theologians have written upon this doctrine, notably, among others, Cardinal Newman and Cardinal Hergenröther; but Dr. Schanz's further words on the point now before us will be regarded as particularly instructive. He says: "Infallible judgments and decisions are not sudden flashes of the mind, nor simple expressions of sovereign and arbitrary will. An *ex cathedra* decision is not an *ex tempore* decision. The Pope, and the bishops in union with him, . . . are obliged to search and inquire, to infer and gather from tradition, present and past, what does and what does not belong to the apostolic deposit. . . . In this process they are so assisted by the divine Spirit that they can only arrive at an infallibly certain definite conclusion."[1] And the Pope's infallibility means that he is "the supreme and final witness." So, if it is asked, *When* does the Holy Father speak *ex cathedra*, and is accordingly infallible? the answer is,—When he speaks as the teacher of all Christians; in the name and with the authority of the apostles; to define a doctrine of faith or morals; and with the purpose of binding the universal Church.

These conditions, plainly laid down in the definition, are essential for its true explanation. The claim which it makes, even with all modification, may be called astounding, we know. It is the highest claim for the judgment of man which can be conceived of, to decide with unerring certainty what is the re-

[1] *Christian Apology*, iii., pp. 534, 546.

vealed truth of God. We might suppose such gift impossible—to be entrenching upon God's own prerogative—were it not for our Lord's words to St. Peter. Upon those words the Church's doctrine rests, as upon an indestructible foundation. But weighty as the claim for the Pope may be made, it is not an unlimited claim. His infallibility pertains to his office, and to that office in definite exercise. It is not his personal opinions, nor his private utterances upon whatever subject, that are infallible; not even his reasons for giving a certain definition; but *the definition—the decision itself*, when he formally proclaims it, with intention to bind the whole Church.

Now what is there unreasonable, it may be confidently asked, in the Church's doctrines of the Pope's primacy and infallibility? We affirm for them eminent reasonableness. And what do we mean by this? That the more they are understood, and in all their bearings, the more they commend themselves to our intelligence. This would not of itself be sufficient ground for accepting them. They might be only beautiful conjectures, plausible hypotheses to account for human inventions. Indeed, that is just what our Protestant friends are apt to throw out—not always with good will—in reference to these cardinal doctrines of the Church's organization. We need say no more now of so false an attitude; we only wish to put the matter of reasonableness in its true light; and all we claim for it is that, while the doctrines must be accepted because they are God's revealed will, this additional consideration is always legitimately kept in mind. God always requires of us a reasonable faith, a reasonable obedience, never the contrary.

As to the Pope's primacy, then, taking for granted the principle of authority, without which the Church could not exist, the provision of visible headship commends itself as in the best sense natural, and as the only way fitted to secure greatest advantages.

A body would naturally have a head, a visible body a visible head. If it be hinted that it is only a figure of speech, anyway, by which the Church is called a body, we know it is a figure continually used, even from apostolic times; and if He Whom all the apostles united in calling the divine Head of the whole Church, visible and invisible, could confer such powers as He did upon one of them, it was natural that he or his successor should very soon come to be called the head of the visible Church wherein he exercised these powers.

Can it be shown that this visible headship interferes with the invisible, heavenly headship of Christ ? In our judgment, so far is this from being true, to the unprejudiced mind it helps to prove that headship. It is really part of it. One may allow for all the sincerity of the Anglican prelates who, in their late reply to the Pope's encyclical, deplore " that error which is inveterate in the Roman communion of substituting the visible head for the invisible Christ "; but only its sincerity can save the complacent ejaculation from being as deplorable as it is untrue. Peter is in the place of Christ, the Pope is Christ's vicegerent —and by His own appointment; but that is a very different thing from the visible being substituted for the invisible—man, however exalted, substituted for God! So if any partisan controversialist exclaims, as one recently has, " Alas! the earthly head, being no part of the institution of Christ, does not reveal the heavenly Head, but hides Him,"[1] we are not surprised that a false premise leads him to a false conclusion. But what if the very opposite ground of belief be the true one? That is precisely our position as Catholics; and thus we can say,—the earthly head does not hide but gloriously reveals the heavenly. Being a part of His institution it must reveal Him. Here is the crowning feature of all the appointments of the visible Church, which, because visible, is ever bearing most efficient witness to the world and glorifying the unseen Lord, the divine Head.

Further, the indispensable advantages provided by this primacy, it may be asserted with all reverence, could have been secured in no other way. Unity was what the divine Lord foreknew would be the pressing need of the apostles and of the Church which they were to teach and govern. Unity, of course, could not but be a certain mark of His divine institution; but here was His way of safeguarding His creation, whose membership was to be made up of free, responsible human beings.

---

[1] Puller's *The Primitive Saints and the See of Rome*, p. 218.*

To establish a centre of unity for the apostolate is surely a reasonable explanation of the grants made to St. Peter. How else could this have been established? And the Pope as the head of the hierarchy perpetuates this centre of unity for the bishops and for the whole Church. Every other advantage of the Church's organization flows from this; and without this all would be disorder and chaos, as the various other attempts at church government more or less fully show. What has it availed,—do any ask? The Pope's primacy, in all its fullness, was meant to avail, and it has availed continually for final unerring decision of questions of faith and morals. This same primacy, through the faithful loyalty to Christ's vicegerent which has ever distinguished Catholic obedience, has all along firmly settled points of discipline. To the Pope there has been privilege of appeal by councils, bishops, clergy, and people; from him there has been no appeal. Moreover, as the Church is in the world, the influence of this heaven-sent power of the primacy has been again and again felt and recognized in the affairs of nations, in bringing about peace between peoples, in protecting the rights and lessening the wrongs of different classes of society. What a broad, deep stream of wisdom and beneficence has flowed out to the world from the long reign of Leo XIII. !

We can not but feel that we have anticipated much that might be written upon the reasonableness of Papal infallibility in the explanation of the doctrine already given. It is hardly necessary to say more to those who admit at all the claim of any divine authority in the Church. The objections which have been made by those who have not clearly seen the range and limitations of this infallibility ought to disappear with a more definite understanding of the subject, even such as could be gained from a careful reading of the Vatican definition. That the Pope should be infallible, as thus explained, is no monstrous bugbear to the imagination, making him equal to God because divinely assisted. The doctrine does bid men appreciate the reality of divine powers and gifts, it does take us to the realm of the supernatural, as may be said of all Catholic teaching, and it is meant to do so. Nor is it an absurdity, requiring, for example, that we should be ourselves infallible before we can give rational assent to it, as Chillingworth used to say about the infallibility of the Church. We repeat, here is a function belonging to the primacy, and if that is reasonable this need give no serious trouble to the candid, intelligent mind. How can the Pope act as supreme teacher of the Church if his decisions upon questions of faith and morals are not final? And how can they be final if not infallible?

This is no attempt to make light of infallibility by explaining away its presumed difficulties. We would not be justly liable to the charge of undue minimizing. We have intended to make the statement of the doctrine as strong as the Church makes it. We have no right to make it any stronger than that. To do so would be trying " to impose upon the faith of others more than what the Church distinctly claims of them "; and Cardinal Newman, whose words these are, has shown in his full, generous, and loyal treatment of this whole subject, [1] that " a moderation of

[1] See his Letter to the Duke of Norfolk, §9, upon "The Vatican Definition."

doctrine, dictated by charity, is not inconsistent with soundness in the faith."

The Church, let it be said in conclusion, is by God's appointment a monarchy, and the Pope is the monarch; but let it also be remembered just what that means,—that it is governed throughout the world by the bishops, with whom the Pope, at their head, shares his authority, laying upon them all that is reasonably possible. Theology teaches that they are " not mere deputies and mouthpieces of the Holy See," but that within their dioceses they " act by a power which is inherent in their office." [1]

Because the Pope is the supreme ruler, it must not be imagined that the great mass of Catholics the world over are continually being exercised and disturbed about what he may do in government. Many Protestants still cherish that strange idea. The Holy Father is not a dictator. How often, it may fairly be asked, are the great body of the faithful brought into direct connection with the supreme power at Rome? Practically, very seldom, if ever. We put up our prayers for his guidance and safety; we thankfully await

[1] Hunter's *Dogmatic Theology*, iii., pp. 389-397.

his benedictions; his wise oversight reaches to the farthest corner of his empire; but, as Cardinal Newman says, " the weight of his hand upon us, as private men, is absolutely unappreciable."[1] The bishops, as the chief members of the hierarchy under him, rule in their domains, and at frequent intervals make known to him the exact condition of the Church and renew their allegiance to him as the chief pastor, Christ's vicegerent on earth.

No; the government of the Catholic Church is not a tyranny, a despotism, " enthralling and crushing the human mind, depriving it of its faculties, commanding it to believe, and forbidding it to think," as some so narrowly seem to suppose. Let all such put away their prejudices and revise their convictions. We are not the Pope's slaves. We are his loyal subjects; he is our supreme ruler under Jesus Christ. We are his docile pupils and learners; he is our supreme teacher of religious truth under the great Teacher Jesus Christ. We are his dutiful children; he is our Holy Father, the father of all the faithful in Christendom, under God our Father in heaven.

[1] *Difficulties of Anglicans*, ii., p. 229.

XII

THE REAL PRESENCE IN THE EUCHARIST—TRANSUBSTANTIATION

THE Church's mysterious teaching upon the Holy Eucharist and her mysterious sacrificial worship present obstacles to many minds in the way of their accepting the Catholic religion. From a merely human point of view that teaching and that worship are unique, amazing, overwhelming. Yet there is a reasonable way of looking at every subject. It is always of use to try to remove ignorance and misunderstanding, and all the more in reference to profound mysteries; and any who reject are really as unreasonable as were those disciples who, when our Lord spoke of giving them His flesh to eat, said, "This is an hard saying, who can hear it?" and turned away from Him, obstinately refusing His explanation. He would not hamper their freedom; He will not hamper ours; yet now, as then, His own gracious power is ready to enlighten men's minds and make willing their hearts.

As the common point of agreement from which we started in our last subject was the idea of authority, however imperfect, so here it may be some notion, however weak or inconsistent, of the sacraments. It is not requisite for our present purpose to discuss the nature of sacraments, how many Christian sacraments there are, or whether any other than this. Nearly all who call themselves Christians observe some kind of a remembrance of the Last Supper of the Lord, and look upon the rite as the most solemn one in their worship. If non-Catholics in general admit even so much, there is at least a standpoint from which they may be willing to look upon the Catholic position. Would that they might inquire and examine without prejudice!

What, then, is the Catholic teaching concerning the Eucharist, the Blessed Sacrament, as it is most commonly called? That teaching is founded upon Holy Scripture, and claims to be the only plain, consistent interpretation of the words of Jesus Christ. As we all know, when He instituted this sacrament and commanded its observance, He said of the bread, "This is My Body," and of the wine, "This is My Blood." The Catholic faith teaches that those words were literally true; and accordingly, that ever since, by the effectual word of His priests—whose priesthood is a part of His own—there is the Real Presence of Christ in this sacrament. This does not mean merely a spiritual presence; nor a presence *with* the bread and the wine; but, as the Church has carefully defined, to avoid all possible mistake, that here there is "truly, really, and substantially the Body and Blood together with the soul and divinity of our Lord Jesus Christ"; and that there is a change of "the whole substance of the bread into the Body, and of the whole substance of the wine into the Blood." This change, so entirely unique, is called Transubstantiation.

Now, whatever difficulty there may be here, it is plain enough what the Church teaches. And every devout Catholic unquestionably accepts this teaching and rejoices in the blessing and comfort which it bestows. Is it, then, as others sometimes say, only a blind faith, an ignorant following of what is forced upon belief? There is no warrant for such an assumption. Deeply mysterious as the teaching is, it has an aspect of reasonableness. We do not mean by this that the change in the elements can be understood, or the nature of Christ's Presence ever imagined; but that, once believing in the divine power and love, it is reasonable to accept the mystery just as the Church puts it before us.

It is the various attempted substitutes for this teaching which are really unreasonable. Glance at these for a moment. They are based upon a virtual denial of Christ's own words, or they amount only to an absurdity. They do not satisfy either the mind or the heart. It is impossible that they should do so. Those who, following the lead of Zwinglius, make Christ's language figurative, are certainly put to great straits. He did not say, " This represents My Body," " This is a figure of My Body," but " This *is* My Body"; and all professed analogies between this text and others where Scripture language is plainly

Various Protestant Theories 103

figurative fail when candidly examined.[1] It has been well observed that He was not here proposing a parable or explaining an allegory, but establishing a new institution which ought to be done in simple terms; and that " no place in Scripture has been found where the sign of the institution received the name of the thing itself [as *e.g.*, ' this bread is My Body,' meaning—' the sign of My Body '] the moment it was instituted, and without any previous preparation."[2] Accordingly these rationalists are left to a denial of the plain meaning of Christ's own words rather than believe a miracle in accepting them. Such a position can hardly be called reasonable, in Christians; but it is that of most Protestants to-day.

The Lutheran way of trying to escape from this dilemma was by what was called *consubstantiation*. Luther avowed he could not deny the presence of Christ in the Eucharist. So

---

[1] See the Abbe Fouard's *Christ the Son of God*, ii., pp. 228, 229; and Cardinal Wiseman's *Lectures on the Catholic Church*, pp. 506-517.

[2] Bossuet's *History of the Variations of Protestant Churches*, bk. ii., § 26, 27.

Christ—he taught—was present *with* the bread. But this was only a more subtle rationalism than the other. With it properly must be coupled the view of those Anglicans who advocate a real presence, but affirm that there is only a sacramental and not a physical change, according to which, as Father Harper so well showed in his controversy with Doctor Pusey, we are asked to believe in a miracle which is absolutely impossible—" a real change which is a change of nothing!"[1] Such is the absurdity to which Lutheranism and Highchurch Anglicanism (so far as we can assign any definite sacramental belief to the latter) seem to be reduced. The position is perhaps more reverent than that of Zwinglianism; it does not appear to deny Christ's words; but it is just as unreasonable, yes, more so. And while each of the two great parties of Protestantism opposed and ridiculed the other, " they proved against each other," as says Bossuet, " that the Church which they had abandoned *had more reason on her side than either of them.*"[2] Was not this true? Is it not true still?

[1] Father Harper's *Peace Through the Truth*, i., p. 239.
[2] *Variations*, etc., bk. ii., § 36.

Meaning of The Real Presence

The Real Presence of Christ in this sacrament, as the Church teaches, is that of His Body and Blood, His soul and divinity,—in other words, His entire presence. And what other presence could there be? Without going into theological explanation—where His Body is, there must be His soul; where His humanity, there His divinity. Our Lord would give us Himself in this mystery of His love. He would renew our spiritual life, would make us sharers in the merits of His death, would unite us to His risen humanity, and thus even grant us to become "partakers of the divine nature" (2 St. Pet., i., 4). So the medium, or method, which is food, received by the body, only appears to be bread, but is really Himself, humanity and divinity, and for the sustenance of our entire being whereby we are made one with Him and granted the surest pledge of life perfected and eternal with Him in heaven. This is as far as we can go in our apprehension; for the mystery is unspeakable and can not be comprehended.

But the Catholic interpretation is wholly reasonable—as we have shown by contrast even the only reasonable interpretation of

Christ's words. The Church's teaching blinks no difficulties, but meets them openly. It boldly proclaims a miracle, an action "altogether miraculous," and "involving"—as says Father Harper—"a greater exercise of the divine omnipotence than creation itself." The substance of the bread and wine is wholly changed into the substance of the Body and Blood of Christ. How can the Real Presence of our Lord be in this sacrament if there is not this change?—hyperphysical and sacramental, but also physical? Did not He say, "This" [which but a moment before was bread] "is" [now] "My Body"? If any exclaim, Impossible! why "impossible," we reply, to the power of God? But again, there is nothing unreasonable in this point of contact between theology and physics. For "truth can not contradict truth," however much, as a recent writer puts it, "one assured truth may modify our convictions and our mode of expression concerning another." There is here no denial of the evidence of the senses, no foundation for general skepticism, as is sometimes asserted. The Church teaches that all the qualities (the *accidents* in the old technical language) of the bread and wine remain unchanged. Quantity, color, shape, taste, etc., are all there as before. Here is the deep mystery—the accidents, the qualities remaining *without their substance*, and that substance changed into the Divine Body and Blood. Here is the trial of our faith; we believe it because God has declared it; but even in this exercise of His omnipotence—"greater than creation itself"—what we believe is neither a mere scholastic distinction between reality and appearances, as some have ignorantly claimed, nor that He has sanctioned an absurdity, as say others. God forbid! An absurdity is impossible to God. However beyond reason, it is not absurd that by His power all the appearances of bread and wine should exist without the substance. The limitations are in our human knowledge and faculties. How weak is our understanding! How little do we know! This Blessed Sacrament is Christ's way of remaining with us in infinite power and love, while He is also in heaven. Is the mystery far beyond us? Most certainly. Yet it is no greater than that of His Incarnation, of which it is the sequel, the continuation. How can those who really accept that mystery stumble at this?

Many points of interest and importance in relation to this great subject our limits allow us only to touch upon. The adoration of the Eucharist is an essential part of Catholic teaching. But if here Christ is really present, why should He not be adored? Is it not reasonable? Instead of pronouncing this idolatry, ought not the refusal of such worship to be called most shocking impiety? And all the accompanying devotion—the reverence of priests celebrating and ministering, the rapt attention of the faithful, the dignity of ceremonial, the beauty of altars, the splendor of vestments—all are meant to be but expressions of inward faith and love, and all are natural to the Catholic mind and heart, because Jesus Christ our Lord is firmly believed to be as really present here as in heaven, and therefore to be worshiped as truly in this Holy Sacrament as we also worship Him in heaven.

Only the consecrating priest receives the Holy Eucharist in both kinds, as it is called. This Catholic usage, which has been observed now for centuries, much disturbs many Protestants, who call it cruelly depriving the people and giving them only a mutilated sacrament. But the Church's rule is reasonable, and will bear full investigation, little as we can enter upon that here. Our Lord's command at the institution does not affect it, for those who received originally were only the apostles, and this rule concerns only the laity. There can be no mutilation of the sacrament (a preposterous charge!), for theology plainly shows that Christ exists whole and entire under either consecrated element. Partly to meet the opposite heresy, and largely for reasons of reverence and convenience, the regulation stands as it does; and one can hardly resist the conviction that only prejudice, and the force of habit, and pride which will not submit to authority must be the strong ground of this common objection.

The question of required frequency of Communion disturbs some minds, as does also that of the necessity of previous confession. As regards Communion, the Church's commandment is, to receive once a year, during the Easter-time, which is conveniently extended over quite a period so that this Easter duty need not be neglected. All this regulation, of a wise lenity, is by some called only laxity. But may not such misinterpret, and be themselves unreasonable? It must be owned—the Catechism of the Council of Trent, that valuable summary of Catholic teaching, brings it before us—that, because the devotion of Christianity's early days grew cold, the Church was led first to decree " at least three times a year," and later " at least once a year," as the rule for communicants. But, as everybody knows, this is only the minimum of required observance—what one is bound to do, not to be cut off from the Church altogether. Such lenity is not laxness; it is in harmony with the divine mercy and forbearance. But such observance is not the common thing among Catholics. Let the fact of the urgent counsels and instructions of the clergy upon this point and the responding regular and often communicating of the laity prove what is the general custom of the faithful in these days.

In reference to confession, with much inconsistency the very opposite criticism is made. Although the Church is just as lenient—for confession is absolutely required but once a year—yet here, because most people confess far oftener, because the benefit of frequent confession is cheerfully recognized by so many, and because no one can worthily receive the Holy Eucharist in a state of mortal sin, objectors, in the face of the Church's law, cry out against her supposed strictness. How often, in some quarters, do Protestants bring it up against the tyranny (!) of priestly compulsion, that Catholics must always go to confession before Communion! But this is certainly a mistake, both of law and of fact; and while frequent confession is the rule, naturally, with those who communicate often, and while the directions of our pastors must vary much, according to their own opinions and the conditions of their people, it is at least safe to say that the intelligent conscience of each communicant is as fully the guide in this matter as the judgment of the priest.

XIII

THE SACRIFICE OF THE MASS

THE Holy Eucharist, according to Catholic teaching, is both a sacrament and a sacrifice. In the latter sense it commonly takes the name of *The Mass*—a word dating from the fourth century, and strictly referring to the religious service. The offering of this sacrifice is held to be the highest act of Christian worship. Just as the old sacrifices of the Mosaic Law were types which looked forward to the Sacrifice of the Cross, so this looks back to that, and is the continuous Sacrifice of the New Law. When Our Lord instituted this Christian rite, in the words, " This is My Body which shall be delivered [literally, ' is broken '] for you," He began His mysterious sacrifice; and in the separate consecration of the Body and the Blood He mystically denoted and accomplished His death. Further, He commanded the perpetual observance of the rite until He should come again, to commemorate His death, and to show forth and plead with God its boundless merits, even as He re-presents them by His eternal priesthood in heaven.

This is what the Church is doing every day in the Mass, which, accordingly, she teaches is a true sacrifice, offered to God in prayer, praise, thanksgiving, and propitiation; that in it He is Himself really both priest and victim, and His priests but act in His name; that it is no bare memorial, but the bloodless and mystical renewal of the One Sacrifice of the Cross; and that the matchless value of this sacrifice redounds, in fruits general and special, for the benefit of the whole Church and of its individual members—not only, therefore, for the living, but for the faithful departed.

These are wonderful claims, it may be said; and we readily admit it. It is a most wonderful subject, this of the Eucharist, in whatever light regarded. This Holy Sacrifice has to do with the very heart and soul of Christian worship; there is no blessing so great, no grace so precious that it may not be gained through its intercessory power; that power, too, reaches beyond all this visible human life into the realm of the unseen world. But is it all so strange? Is it any way unreasonable? "Men may blaspheme the Christian mysteries," says Padre Agostino, "when they understand them not; may call them strange when superficially regarded; but when they are well studied and considered, we see that they come from the heart of the God-Man, to raise our own hearts to God."[1]

Not professing to enter into full proof of what is claimed for the Mass, but only to present certain points for consideration,—what is there strange, we ask, that Christianity, as well as every other religion, should have its sacrifice? And where else, if not here, is that pure Offering, foretold by prophecy (Malachi, i., 11), made to God in every place among the Gentiles? It is all mystical, and so, deeply mysterious; but is its genuineness thereby destroyed? The One Offering upon the Cross is not repeated; it can not be; but this mystical death by the consecration upon the altar is just as real a sacrifice, though bloodless. Christ does not actually shed His blood nor

[1] *Conferences*, ii., p. 256.

die; yet we can understand how, by His literal presence here, there is a true renewal, a perpetuation of that Sacrifice of the Cross. Here as there, He is both priest and victim. When, therefore, in the Mass, the priest truly offers Christ to His Eternal Father, not only is it the highest worship of prayer and praise and thanksgiving, but it must also be a sacrifice of propitiation—wherein, pleading His infinite merits, we may surely hope to obtain forgiveness of our sins and remission of the punishment due to them, if, as the Church bids us, "with a true heart and right faith, with fear and reverence, contrite and penitent we approach to God."[1] This is not derogating in the least from the Sacrifice consummated on the Cross; it is honoring and exalting that Sacrifice, with which the Mass is essentially one.

Not only has the Mass such power as is claimed for it in behalf of the living; it is to be remembered that it is also available for the dead. It seems strange that there should be the strong prejudice which there has been on this point with many Protestants. What is

[1] Council of Trent: Session xxii., cap. 2.

there unreasonable that "those who are departed in Christ and who are not as yet fully purified" can have this Sacrifice offered for them, as well as that it should be offered "for the sins, punishments, satisfactions and other necessities of the faithful who are alive"? Certainly the Sacrifice has power to reach them, and their needs may be great. Why should it not avail to purify them, already pardoned, and to make them sooner fit for the Beatific Vision in heaven? So thought holy Monica, dying, who entreated St. Augustine, "Lay my body anywhere—only remember me at the Lord's altar";[1] and so have thought vast numbers not so holy as she, who with her have equally believed in the efficacy of that One Offering to fit them for the all-pure presence of God. Right thankful may we be that there is such a "tradition of the apostles" as this, and that the Church has always followed it. To take it away would be to destroy a most precious part of our Christian heritage. It is not necessary here to introduce any defence of prayer for the departed. We only claim that so to pray is an instinct of the

[1] St. Augustine's *Confessions*, bk. ix., cap. xi., 27.

Christian heart. Many, who would not formally admit as much, we are sure do not crush out this instinct; and those who cherish it at all should not wonder that this great and most worthy Sacrifice can be "rightly offered," even as the Church teaches, for this end. In every Mass there is this commemoration of the dead,—of all God's servants "who have gone before us with the sign of faith and sleep the sleep of peace." And that among individual intentions requiem Masses for the departed should be continually offered is a most merciful provision. If the souls in purgatory are helped by the prayers of the faithful, shall not this most mighty prayer, this awful, mystic Sacrifice, the Holy Mass, avail very much?

The relations which the Mass has with the departed present yet another aspect; and here certainly it appeals to Christian gratitude, fellowship, and aspiration. For it is often celebrated, we know, in honor and memory of the saints; not offered to them, but to God alone, that, as St. Augustine says, "we may give thanks to Him for their victories, and may stir up ourselves to imitate them by seeking to obtain like crowns and palms."[1] Believing, too, in their intercession, here we take precious comfort from our faith, as we pray that "they may vouchsafe to intercede for us in heaven whose memories we celebrate on earth."

It follows from what has been said in this paper that the Holy Sacrifice is just the same in all its essentials if there be no worshippers present but the priest. There are the priest, the victim, the altar; and the Sacrifice offered to God, with intention general or special, avails for its legitimate purposes. There is then, strictly, no such thing as a private Mass. And yet in this connection it must be said that the duties of the people in this regard are most plainly laid down. They are explicitly bidden to hear Mass on Sundays and holydays of obligation, and this is one of the few express commandments of the Church. The requirement is eminently reasonable. They assist by their devout presence in this holy service (for it is no mere idle, listless "hearing" which the precept enjoins); they "offer with the priest the Holy Sacrifice." The

[1] *City of God*, bk. viii., 27.

priest offers " as Christ's minister and in His person; and the people by the hands of the priest." This is why their presence is insisted upon. This is why Catholics go to Mass. It is their duty and their privilege. They are not, as some seem to think, like dumb beasts going through with a perfunctory routine. They are intelligent receivers of a precious gift, intelligent offerers of a sacrifice, in the sincere worship of their hearts. They belong to the " holy priesthood " of all the faithful (1 St. Peter, ii., 5); and it is the glory of the Catholic Church that it really recognizes this priesthood, and insures its blessings in obedience; while those who, in a spirit of independence of God's appointments, say so much about " the priesthood of the people," know not of what they speak, and in prejudice or wilfulness fail of the blessings.

The language, the Latin, used in the service of the Mass, admits of rational explanation. It is ancient, long established, and fixed in meaning. Just because it is not a living language that meaning is not continually liable to change. Ought there not to be here, if anywhere, that rigid conservatism which will be the best safeguard for the fixed truth? The difficulties from its use in worship, though real, and not to be contemptuously ignored, are by no means equal, from a reasonable point of view, to those which would certainly arise from the use of the vernacular. The use of a tongue "understanded of the people" was a popular outcry at the Reformation which had some sense from the standpoint of malcontents, but which evidently involved false issues. The Mass is certainly not "common prayer," in the Protestant sense, and is not meant to be. On the other hand, the positive advantage of the Latin, in dignity and beauty and adaptation to its high use, may be more and more manifest to those who will try to give up prejudice and look at the matter from the Catholic standpoint.

The great difficulty in all minds which find serious obstacles to the Catholic religion in connection with the Holy Eucharist, as sacrament or sacrifice, arises from the truth of the Real Presence. Let this be once apprehended, by faith accepted and firmly held, and all else legitimately follows. Worship, offering, propitiation, benefits received prayed for or hoped for, for ourselves or others, in time or eternity, all are bound up in this central truth. Its acceptance is the key to the deep peace, the manifest joy, the earnest devotion of Catholic congregations. But if this truth is denied or doubted, how can other claims be admitted? They should not be; they mean but superstition and idolatry. But who can doubt or deny, without rejecting Christ's own words? There they stand,—"This is My Body"; "This is My Blood." It is reasonable to accept them, with all their mystery, because they are the words of God Himself. It is unreasonable to reject them, to cavil over them or seek to explain them away, and think to call ourselves Christians.

Meanwhile the need, the great need of Jesus Christ, *His Real Presence* in sacrament and sacrifice, to be fed upon for the soul's life and strength, to be offered to God for His honor and the unspeakable good of men, is throughout Christendom being largely ignored. "The nations are troubled and the people are convulsed, because Jesus is no longer with them." More and more free-thought in religion is bearing sway over men's minds; and free-thought in religion leads in its train theories, customs, practices destructive of morality and ominous of disaster to individual, social, national life. The beginning was in throwing off allegiance to this truth which the Blessed Sacrament alone conserves, which the Mass alone proclaims. Let the disobedient return to the unity of the Church, and gain a strength, a comfort, a reality in religion which now they can not know. The world's unrest will find its true remedy only in loving submission to God's truth in all its fulness; and this is nowhere seen but in the Catholic faith.

XIV

THE PLACE OF THE BLESSED VIRGIN IN THE CATHOLIC SYSTEM

But what does the Catholic Church teach about the Blessed Virgin? ask many eager questioners; and what of the remarkable devotion to her? She holds the highest place accorded to any creature,—is the answer, in a word. Belief and devotion rest upon an unquestioned fact in her history, upon the inferences which have grown out of that fact in the development of the Church's tradition from earliest times, and upon the resulting dogma promulgated in our own day—her Immaculate Conception. To the Catholic mind this belief and devotion appear to be in the truest sense natural, the only Christian position to take, and, if one believes at all in the divine origin of Christianity, the only common-sense position.

Yet upon no subject does there seem to be

more persistent misunderstanding and prejudice among Protestants. Citing the free, emotional language of devotion (and there must be wide liberty in devotion—it is a Catholic principle), they still cry out against "Mariolatry"; or, if they touch upon the subject theoretically, there will be some such utterance as recently fell from an able and broad-minded Protestant journal, that "the worship of the Virgin Mary is the worship of the element of womanliness in God";—most ridiculous!—for, in the Protestant sense, we do not "worship" the Virgin Mary at all; and as for "the element of womanliness in God," Catholic belief knows no such thing, and would brand the notion as abominable as it is absurd. Is all this the Christian intelligence of (almost) the twentieth century? we ask in surprise; either narrow bigotry (which, we are thankful, is somewhat disappearing), or sickly apology thinking mildly to philosophize, but lacking the rudiments of knowledge! It is evident there is need of more light upon the subject; and to show, but a little, the reasonableness of Catholic teaching and practice is the aim of this paper. We do not hope to convince the wilful who are intelligent; but we would try to keep their wilful intelligence from deluding others.

The Virgin Mary, whom all generations, as she predicted, are calling " Blessed," is the Mother of Our Lord. And who is Our Lord? That is really the first and trying point of difficulty to many non-Catholic minds. The spirit of Unitarian rationalism, so largely prevalent, is ready to own Him a very good man, the best man, even the divine man; but the Catholic faith has always taught Him to be the God-Man, none other than God Himself, who, " conceived by the Holy Ghost," took our human nature—body and soul—in the womb of the Virgin Mary. Accordingly, as this is His true personality, she is, even as the Third General Council declared her, " the Mother of God." This conclusion is as reasonable as it is irresistible; and to the intelligent mind there seems to be need of no further words upon this topic.

If, then, the Blessed Virgin is the Mother of God, what sinless purity must we ascribe to her! What grace may we not believe was shown to her, manifested in her! Can we presume that the Son of God would be born of one with the least stain of sin? Could He be what He is, in the perfection of His humanity, if He were so born? Would He not, then, have prepared her, in body and soul, to become His Mother? That is certainly a most reasonable inference; and it carries with it the whole truth concerning the sanctity of the Blessed Virgin.

How far back does this sanctity reach? The Church claims it reaches to the first moment of her existence; in other words, that her conception was immaculate, that she was "preserved from the stain of original sin." And clearly no less an idea of her purity can satisfy the conditions of her divine maternity. Nor is there here any contradiction of Scripture, which tells of Christ coming in the likeness of sinful flesh, which declares that all have sinned and fallen, are included in the curse pronounced upon Adam, and need the redemption of Jesus Christ. Mary's nature which she inherited from her parents was not different from ours. She was a real child of Adam, and was redeemed by the blood of Christ. As Cardinal Newman states it, "We

Mary's Sinlessness

consider that in Adam she died, as others; that she was included, together with the whole race, in Adam's sentence; that she incurred his debt, as we do; but that, for the sake of Him Who was to redeem her and us upon the cross, to her the debt was remitted by anticipation,"[1] etc.

And with this must be connected the fulness of grace which was bestowed upon her. What is called original sin is, according to all Catholic teaching, a state or condition—one which consists in the deprivation of that grace which was given our first parents at their creation, and which they lost by disobedience. This grace was granted the Blessed Virgin. Well might the Fathers call her the second Eve, who by obedience was the means of restoring to the race what the disobedience of the first Eve lost. She was indeed "full of grace." From the very first instant of her conception, her soul was pure, and thus by grace sustained, could contract no taint from the body—which by inheritance from Adam must still be called "flesh of sin"—but even kept the body itself pure; and so, through

[1] *Difficulties of Anglicans*, ii., p. 48.

that immaculate conception, the whole being began an existence free from the least stain of sin.

And when she was born, and as she went on in life, what is there to forbid our believing that she was kept wholly sinless? Could not that same grace which granted her a sinless conception grant her power to lead a sinless life? And does not the one reasonably follow the other as the fit condition of her who became the Virgin Mother of God? For, as St. Augustine says, who will allow no mention of her where sin is concerned—she is the one exception among saints—"how do we know what increase of grace was bestowed on her to enable her to overcome sin in every way, who merited to conceive and bring forth Him who had no sin?"[1]

All these inferences from the fact of her Divine Motherhood—inferences which establish her sinless conception and life—are believed by Catholics to be implicitly contained in Scripture. The germ of the dogma of the Immaculate Conception is in the apostolic deposit of revelation. Very early it began to

[1] *On Nature and Grace*, ch. xxxvi.

The Immaculate Conception

develop in liturgies—emphatically in the Eastern Church,[1] and soon in homilies of the Fathers throughout East and West. Tradition more and more established the true meaning of Scripture. For a considerable period, in later centuries, while the doctrine was an open question, it was even matter of violent controversy, and among great scholars and divines, St. Bernard, St. Thomas, St. Bonaventure, St. Anselm, Scotus, Suarez and others — names which we mention because sundry of them are often quoted by Protestants as diametrically opposed to the extreme ideas of what they call "modern Romanism," whereas these same men were the stanch defenders of the sinlessness of the Blessed Virgin, only, as their discussions show, many aspects of the doctrine of her conception were not, could not be, as well understood then as later. But all this contention of authorities need not surprise us. As a careful writer upon the subject observes, "This is the ordinary law of doctrinal growth. Divine truths

[1] Are all of our Anglican friends who are looking for affiliation in that direction fully acquainted with these liturgies upon this point?

are evolved amidst the conflict of schools, and show their supernatural life and origin by gradually casting off all that is heterogeneous, and fixing themselves, in the ever-increasing light of their evidence, on the consciousness of the Church."[1] And so it was with this revealed doctrine, which, at last, in its explicit fulness, took its place forever in the Creed of the Church by that solemn definition of Pius IX. in 1854.

There are many lights in which this recent definition may be viewed. One, certainly, is its value, in these days of humanitarianism, as an additional safeguard of the truth of the Incarnation. Long ago was Mary declared by the Church to be the Mother of God. Now she is declared sinless. Those who misunderstand or deny say we are thus dishonoring Jesus Christ; but it is the very opposite, we are honoring Him. If there were any taint of sin in her, it might be questioned in reason, who He is; but now there can be no question. The newly defined truth is "for the exaltation of the Catholic faith and the spread of the Christian religion." More and more will it be

[1] Father Harper's *Peace Through the Truth*, i., pp. 383, 400.

found that they who thus honor the Blessed Virgin are they who honor her divine Son, while they who refuse her this honor either have no faith in Him as God, or are, however unconsciously, taking sides with such as have not that faith, and so giving aid to the deniers of the central truth of Christianity. In the unrest of our times is not this a condition of things which those who still profess faith in Christ should carefully consider?

Catholic devotion to the Blessed Virgin flows naturally from the purity and dignity which the Church believes are hers. The broad principle of the veneration of the saints, the efficacy of their intercession, and the benefit of our invoking them we do not now speak of at length, hoping to make all this the subject of a later paper. But taking for granted the general truth, we may now give it special application. If any saint is to be venerated, shall it not be the holy Mother of God? What power or privilege can we assign to any creature of which she is not worthy? Here, then, is the root of the Church's devotion. She is singularly exalted, above angels, above all other saints, in the heavenly glory. She is more than all others near and dear to her divine Son, Who has borne His humanity with Him into the heavens. There reigning with Him (do not the saints reign with Christ in heaven ?) we pay her the high honor which is her due. But does this lessen our devotion to Jesus Christ? Catholics claim it strengthens and increases that devotion. The two are entirely different. We venerate her; we adore Him. While there is a permitted wide range of devotional expression to the Virgin, and while some may go beyond lawful bounds, all know that it is " an impassable distance which separates her from the excellence and dignity of the Son of God, her Child."[1]

Yet, in a most true sense, very near Him she is; and thus she, who is so near Him, is also brought into close and precious relations with us. As He is our great Mediator, she among the saints becomes our chief human intercessor. Bearing upon her heart the salvation of the world which He has redeemed, knowing from Him, as we may reverently believe, the needs of this and every land and time, what more natural than that she should

[1] Father Harper, i., p. 325.

intercede for us; and if we pray for each other and ask others to pray for us, is it not reasonable—as it is scriptural—that we should invoke her intercession? The burden of petition, as in the *Hail Mary*, is "Pray for us." Here too, however, Catholics enjoy large freedom. "Intercession is one thing," remarks Cardinal Newman, "devotion is another." It is good and useful, teaches the Church, to ask her prayers; "natural and prudent for those to have recourse to her, who from the Church's teaching know her power"; they make no mistake who frequently and statedly put up such petitions; let us presume it is the rule with Catholics in the exercise of their freedom; but the Church goes no farther than recommendation; and it is an utter mistake, if not a base slander, to say, as some have said, that moral compulsion is ever brought to bear upon Catholics to cause them to invoke the Blessed Virgin. As regards her intercession, sometimes it is spoken of as "omnipotent"; but that common Catholic expression can be readily explained without taking it literally. Sometimes she is called "the way to Jesus, as Jesus is the way to the

Father"; but it would be the abuse of such a comparison to make it mean that we should go to Mary *instead* of going to Jesus, or that we *must* go to her as the only way of access to Him.

Catholic teaching concerning the Blessed Virgin, the more it is candidly looked into, shows her in a most remarkable way combining qualities which appeal to reverence and affection. She is next to God—His highest, noblest creature—but she is the fellow-creature of the lowest of us. She is the most exalted saint in heaven, receiving homage from all the faithful, but she is also our Mother—so given from the cross to us—and she follows all her children with a mother's care and love. Thus she would have us regard her, and remember her human heart as well as her sublime prerogatives. If the saints in heaven know what takes place on earth, this Virgin Mother must be well aware of the feverish unrest, the unsatisfied longing in the midst of which we live, and in which perforce we more or less share. She knows the misery of proud men who will not enter the House of the True Faith, but go on building their Babels of mental, moral, and social confusion. She knows all this, and she intercedes for us all. In God's good time may the world better understand her benign mission, and appreciate the relation which her sinlessness, her dignity, her intercession have to all our needs and aspirations! As really one of us she comes even nearer to us than we have yet said. The model particularly for Christian women, maidens or mothers, she is the ideal woman of the race, the example to all in purity and humility. Her influence in forming noble Christian character during all these centuries can not be estimated.

In none of the aspects of her earthly or heavenly life can she be separated in our thought from Jesus Christ, her divine Son. She leads inevitably to Him. All her gifts of grace are from His infinite merits. As woman and as saint, as example and as advocate, Him she continually honors. Is it not time that all this were fairly, fully recognized?—time, at least, that all Christian people no longer hesitated to accord her her rightful place in belief and devotion?

XV

HOW THE CHURCH TREATS SIN

CHRISTIANITY presupposes the fact of sin. Whether the Son of God would have become the Son of Man if there had been no sin from which to redeem the world is a question which was once much discussed. Practically it is a useless question. Sin explains the Incarnation.

Viewed either as the creature's revolt against the Creator's rightful authority, or as a malignant disease spreading corruption, sin is here, within us and all about us. It can not be denied any more than our existence. Those who will not admit the revolt against God know neither God nor themselves. Such are smothering conscience, God's voice within them. All men are forced to own the evil, the disease, in the world; and the most complacent moralist whose deeds abound in natural goodness can not say the root of the evil is not in himself. Those who can look about upon the conditions of life, in families, in society, in the state, under the highest as well as the lowest grade of civilization, and then try to explain away the evil they see, or call it by some smoother name than sin—only an accident or a mistake, which education and progress are surely disposing of—such are themselves deceivers or deceived, proclaiming an optimism as false as it is superficial.

All fanciful theories of this sort are of no avail. The great heart of humanity throbs true, and disdains them. It well knows there is no use in pretending joy and peace where there is so much sorrow and strife. The world is in unrest, and to-day more than ever because of sin. The fact is evident, from the world's growing worse as well as better; and more and more, we believe, is the world so feeling it. Vast numbers would own it who now do not, but that they are looking in vain for an effectual remedy. People have been told so long either that they have no sin, that there is no such thing as sin—the teaching of pure naturalism; or else that it is no matter how much they sin—the result of Luther's false theories; their heads have been so filled with sentimental talk or their minds so shaken with sensational fears; they have so yielded to their crude imaginings or their subtle philosophizings (it makes little difference which) generation after generation for more than three hundred years, following what their private judgment got out of the Bible or in spite of the Bible, with no voice of authority to guide or interpret, to rebuke or comfort, that for one or other of these reasons they are slow to own that there can be any such voice to tell them truly what will bring them even now peace from their unrest, and hereafter the perfect peace of eternity.

There is such a voice, such a message. They are from the Church which Christ established, and which has never ceased, as part of its message, to tell men of sin and its remedy. The Church's life and growth, the transformations which it has wrought in human character, prove what a power this voice has had. But are there not multitudes outside the Church, Christian or non-Christian people, whose need is what we have just described? Will they ever come in, or to any great extent? Verily such a result may be no vain prediction, if we read aright the uneasiness of our times. There is a stir, a movement, in the confused mass of men; it is chiefly in one direction; we are reminded of Froude's striking words, —" In proportion to the depth with which men feel sin they will gravitate towards Rome,"—and we ask ourselves, Is this the effect we see ? Is here one of many causes ?

Only an outline, at best, of the Church's way of treating sin can be presented in these pages. Moral theology, so-called, is a vast domain of itself, with bounds as wide as human nature. The most we can here do is to state certain prominent points of Catholic teaching and practice, try to dispel ignorance and prejudice concerning them, and show with what reasonableness they appeal to the general needs of men.

First of all, then, the Church teaches the dread reality of sin. It is the only evil she knows in this fair world of God's creation; but this evil is stupendous, a huge blot upon God's work, a great " primal disorder " reaching back to the disobedience of our first ancestors and involving all their descendants, with whom sin is, as it always has been, "something personal, conscious, voluntary," and consists, more than in overt acts, in the thoughts of the heart.

As another matter of fundamental teaching, the Church points always to the precious sacrifice of Christ, and claims that only through its infinite merits can the guilt of sin be pardoned, its defilement removed, its punishment averted. These infinite merits of Christ are applied to us by means which Himself has appointed, in holy sacraments. Baptism is the sacrament of regeneration, in which the soul is new-born, the past of sin original or actual is washed away, and a fresh life begun as pure as that of paradise. The Holy Eucharist, primarily for continuing the spiritual life through the Body and Blood of Christ, is also a sacrament of pardon.

But there is another sacrament, that of Penance, particularly appointed for this purpose— for the pardoning and cleansing away of all sin after baptism. As baptism can not be repeated, this sacrament holds a most important place in Catholic teaching and practice. The authority for it is found in the power which

Our Lord gave His apostles to forgive or to retain sin and the promise He connected with it. "Whose sins ye shall forgive, they are forgiven them, and whose sins ye shall retain, they are retained." Here let us clear up one possible difficulty at the outset. It is God, it is Christ, Who forgives. The minister of this, as of all sacraments, only acts in Christ's name. His power, therefore, real as it is, is a deputed power. Now since he is appointed so to act, it is a kind of tribunal or place of judgment which the Church in this sacrament sets up. But how can the priest, who is the judge in the tribunal, be able to give judgment unless the sinner, who is both accuser and accused, reveal his sins? This is the ground for confession, in itself; and on the face of it it is reasonable, for it is necessary. The sinner, with sincere sorrow for his sins and resolve to sin no more, confesses to the priest as to God, and receives God's pardon.

But various objections arise in the non-Catholic mind. What need of confession to the priest? Because Christ has so authorized, and His Church (acting infallibly) has from the first so taught,—must be the answer. But does not God bid us come directly to Him? And who says you shall not?—we reply. Can you take up any Catholic manual of prayers without finding such coming to God taught and encouraged? It is a part of prayer, and no one would think of leading the Christian life without such freedom. But this is not saying you should not also go to God in confession and for pardon through His priest as He has commanded. Perfect contrition— sorrow for sin and detestation of it from supreme love for God—the Church teaches it is possible for you to exercise, and this always gains His instant and entire pardon; but one item of such contrition would naturally be your desire to obey all God's ordinances, and this is one of them, " the ordinary means of conveying remission of sin; . . . and what is extraordinary and purely internal should not be allowed to dispense with the use of the ordinary and external means of attaining the same end."[1] But how can the priest know I am contrite, and sufficiently so? He can not know, of course, but that you are a hypocrite; only in such case your absolution

[1] Father Hunter's *Dogmatic Theology*, iii., p. 321.

is of no worth, for we can not deceive God; and as for the degree of contrition, it may be very imperfect, so it is sincere. God knows; He judges; and He is merciful to every honest soul which so desires His pardon as to submit to His ordinances,—and even if fear of punishment as well as love for Him be part of the motive.

The element of shame, the humiliation of confessing one's sins to a fellow-man, however good and holy, enters largely into the objections made. The proud heart rises against it. Yet even this objection is not so powerful as it seems to be. It is more than counterbalanced by the good to our nature of just this humiliation; by the counsel and help which thousands upon thousands own they have gained from this sacrament, and could have gained in no other way; by the sympathy, so human, yet breathing a divine charm, which the soul receives; and more than all else by the pardon which the priest pronounces in Christ's name. Well does the Council of Trent speak of the calming, consoling effect of that human voice, "heard even as that of Christ the Lord," as one great object which He had in view in mercifully appointing this sacrament. Further, all sins are safely confided to the priest. The hidden sin —before known only to one's own self and God—the base, bold, horrible, revolting sin, all are kept by him, under strictest obligations, even at risk of life, a sure secret. This is no fancy of imagination; it is simple fact, with hardly a single exception in the whole history of the Church. The seal of the confessional is inviolate. No court of justice tries to extort knowledge, from this source, of even the most dreadful crime. Moreover, highest legal authorities have again and again decided that it is for the true welfare of society as well as for the best interests of individual morality that such secrets be sacredly kept.

So much is still left unsaid upon this important topic of confession that we must postpone it to our next paper, which will also take up the punishment of sin, with a few words upon indulgences.

XVI

A FEW WORDS MORE UPON AN IMPORTANT SUBJECT

IT is often wondered at or criticized among non-Catholics that the Church should distinguish as she does between sin and sin. But such distinction is reasonable. Other systems regard all as alike, and so tend to make either too much or too little of sin, with frequent results of either despair or carelessness in the sinner. The Church says some sins are grievous, mortal—cutting off from God and bringing spiritual death, while others are light and so venial—the failings of our weak nature, which in themselves do not deprive of God's grace. We need not here illustrate this distinction. In determining which are mortal, which venial, the motive is always particularly considered, and no sin is deemed so great that it can not be pardoned.

Nor does the Church make any distinction

which denies that the essence of all sin is the same. Venial sins, she says, may lead to mortal sins, and so, though it is obligatory to confess only the latter, it is held to be useful also to confess the former. Such as do so need not imagine, as is sometimes claimed, that they have lost their freedom. That is a foolish whim. Everybody can see, from the rule we have just mentioned, how wide a liberty is enjoyed. No one's conscience is in the hands of the priest. We do not confess our sins to him solely for the sake of confessing them, nor at all—as some fancy—that we may have a clean record and begin to sin again, but that, by stern self-discipline and through the grace of the sacrament which Christ has appointed, we may gradually forsake them, conquer them, destroy them. What the priest wants to do is to strengthen conscience, not to weaken it; and however much may be made of what is called "direction," this is the aim of every wise confessor. "It is impious," declares the Council of Trent, "to call confession a slaughter-house of consciences; for it is certain that nothing else is required of penitents but that, after each has examined himself diligently, . . . he confess those sins by which he shall remember that he has mortally offended his Lord and God." No! the Church in her treatment of sin wisely does not attempt the impossible. "She has no warrant," as Cardinal Newman truly says, "and she has no encouragement, to enforce upon men in general more than those habits of virtue, the absence of which would be tantamount to their separation from God; and she thinks she has done a great deal, and exults in her success, does she proceed so far; and she bears as she may what remains still to be done, in the conviction that, did she attempt more, she might lose all."[1]

It can not be denied that there have been abuses in connection with confession. What good thing has not been abused? Here is a contact, most close and peculiar, of human nature with human nature. In spite of all the safeguards which the Church provides, there are opportunities. Yet all that can possibly be said justly weighs but as the dust in the balance. Abuses, positive or negative, are chiefly the magnifying of a few sad in-

[1] *Difficulties of Anglicans*, i., p. 245.

stances, and exist mostly in the books and minds of ultra-protestants or open unbelievers. The confessional is really a bulwark of all right living, the strength of which can hardly be overestimated. This is emphatically to be said of it in its development of holiness among the faithful. But its worth does not end thus. Imagine the confessional everywhere silenced, this healing, restoring sacrament destroyed— there would be a most baneful revival of sin throughout the world. Sin as a power among men—to whatever you trace it—is thus held in control, and to an extent we can perhaps little credit who know of the enormities of paganism only by what we read about them.

Yet the root of the matter is not reached by saying,—well, it may be better to let confession stay, for the good of those who have been brought up that way! This concession covers but half the ground. The Church is aggressive, and has a gospel for all men. Is the Protestant world any better, we ask, or as good, without this sacrament of Penance? Too largely is it true that there is either a making light of sin, or else a morbid dread of its consequences which leads to despair. We do not question the noble, earnest Christian characters of thousands of people about us in every walk of life; but for all that, there is too often a covering up of sin, or ridiculing it, or glorying in it, from fashion, or custom, or even education,—or else, when conscience protests, a smothering of that divine voice, and a rushing to all lengths of sin or a sinking into utter despondency; all which manifestations are a part of the signs of our times and show the world's unrest. And all this the Church's method of dealing with sin, honestly accepted, would control and remedy.

As to the punishment of sin, the Church teaches that those who leave this life under the guilt of actual grievous sin are punished eternally. The gravity of this teaching forbids our here doing much more than simply to state it. Only a full presentation of it could be satisfactory. But it is based upon language of revelation so clear and strong that Catholics believe it can not be explained away any more than the eternity of heaven. This teaching magnifies God's justice; yes, in spite of all the prejudice which makes of God only a Being of weak benevolence, it magnifies also His love and mercy. Could men understand more the heinousness of wilful sin in God's sight, they would see that it is not reasonable to expect such sin should ever enter heaven; and if they would but remember how reasonable is His limiting the time of repentance to this life, and that He will mercifully reckon every lack of knowledge or opportunity, they would, even under the motive of fear—a motive quite legitimate—give up captious fault-finding with God's government, and devote themselves to escaping hell and gaining heaven. This is what the Church would have them do. Moreover, her doctrine of eternal punishment, stern as it is, is not the unmitigated horror which much of Protestantism—for example, Calvinism—proclaims, a reaction from which has so largely caused the denial of the doctrine altogether. Catholic teaching tells, besides, of purgatory,—not much, indeed, authoritatively, but that there is after death such a place of cleansing from all venial sins, and of temporal punishment for sins the guilt of which has been forgiven but not fully expiated in this life.

The satisfaction which the priest enjoins in

the sacrament of Penance is partly of the nature of such punishment. In the early days of the Church this satisfaction, or outward penance, was often very severe, going to the extreme of personal humiliation and degradation. The milder method of our times has much to be said in its favor, while it preserves the principle; for still as much as ever the priest is the judge who affixes such penalty as is "salutary and convenient according to the quality of the sins and the powers of the penitent."

But the principle has a wider application. It reaches to fastings and prayers and alms and other works of piety voluntarily undertaken; and particularly, it may be said, it includes the bearing with patience whatever trials God sends upon us in this life. Worthy Catholics consecrate their sufferings to God, and pray that they may be accepted for Christ's sake. For all these trials, the Church teaches, are satisfactions for our sins which God does accept through the merits of Christ. The dignity which is thus given to suffering, and the strength to suffer, are found nowhere else. If, as another pertinently says, "sin must have its punishment, and we all must suffer, . . . what a new light is cast on the history of the soul, what a change is made in our judgment of the external world, what a reversal of our natural wishes and aims for the future! . . . He who believes that suffer he must and that delayed punishment may be greater, will be above the world, will admire nothing, fear nothing, desire nothing. He has within his breast a source of greatness, self-denial, heroism."[1] The ground for a claim like this is really not far to seek, though at first it may seem strange to some. All such suffering, borne by the Christian with patience and resignation to God's will, helps to that cleansing of the soul which God knows we need, even in this life lightens the burden of the future, and goes to make the eternal future sure.

And what of purgatory, and its certainly severe suffering? That is the place of temporal punishment, the state of cleansing discipline through which those saved souls must pass who are not, when called from earth, perfectly fit for God's all-holy Presence. The

[1] Newman's *Essay on Development*, p. 394.

conscience of man bears striking witness that most souls are not so fitted. The perfect saints at death are comparatively very few. Is purgatory a hard doctrine? Rightly understood it is reasonable, and the more it is thought of it is consoling and strengthening. All who reach purgatory are safe, safe forever. Sin is not there, nor temptation. Even if the Blessed Vision of God is absent, His grace is there in all its fulness, to prepare for that Vision and that Presence throughout eternity. How long any may be detained there we can not know. Time is not, and one day is as a thousand years. We only know, from Scripture and tradition, what the Church tells us, that the holy souls there are helped by the prayers of the faithful on earth. Here again the Church shows herself in close touch with human nature. Her teaching is not an idle superstition. Death is no barrier between souls. Militant on earth or suffering in that intermediate state, all are united in the one great communion of the faithful. Can we cease to pray for the departed in the Lord, and especially to offer at the hands of His priest the Holy Sacrifice of the altar, for the repose of their souls and their speedy entrance into heaven?

In this connection a few words must be said upon indulgences. An indulgence is a remission of temporal punishment in this life or in purgatory. To say that this remission can, of course, avail only for those whose grievous sins are pardoned, is itself sufficient answer to the false charge that an indulgence is a license to commit sin—a charge so absurd as well as so base that we should not mention it, but that some continue to bring it up, from ignorance or malice. The Church's power to grant indulgences is correctly inferred from her power of "binding and loosing" which Christ Himself bestowed, and their reasonableness depends upon the fact that the merits of Christ are infinite, constituting a kind of "treasury" (an expressive word, but much misunderstood), to which may be added the merits of at least some of the saints.

All that the Church further defines upon the subject is that the use of indulgences is salutary; and when the conditions are taken into account and the hoped-for result, who can deny this? "As to their effect in detail," as Father Hunter and every other theologian would affirm, "nothing can be known." The principle is a generous one: and the doctrine in its right application helps, not hinders, Christian living. For many centuries pope after pope has liberally granted them to various prayers and devotions and charitable works; and the cause of true religion has been thereby strengthened. Every intelligent Catholic (and all should strive to be such) would admit the abuses in the past, "flagrant and too frequent"—to quote Cardinal Wiseman— "through the avarice and rapacity and impiety of men; especially when indulgence was granted to the contributors towards charitable or religious foundations."[1] It is a patent fact of history that Luther made indulgences the ground of his separation from the Church; though many have forgotten, if they ever knew, how, beginning with contending against an abuse, he went on insolently to attack the whole doctrine and practice. As for abuses, the Church was all along trying to remedy them. Many popes and councils strongly condemned them; notably the Council of

[1] *Lectures on the Catholic Church*, p. 417.

Trent, whose decree recommending "that moderation be observed in granting indulgences, lest, by excessive facility, ecclesiastical tradition be enervated," took these various abuses seriously in hand, and effected a complete reform.

Thus much it has seemed necessary to say, if anything, upon a subject which, partly from obscurity of terms and partly from the difference between ancient and modern church-life, has been largely misunderstood, and too often wilfully misrepresented. There is nothing unreasonable about indulgences, nothing to cause fairly the sneer or the shudder with which Protestantism has pointed at them. Indulgences will be only a source of good to such as gain them,—not always so easy a matter as some imagine. If punishment of sin is thereby remitted, or the pain of purgatory thereby lessened or shortened, it is a cause of thankfulness to the mercy of God which so abounds in His Church.

XVII

MERIT, AS THE CHURCH TEACHES IT

THE Christian doctrine of merit affirms that by God's help we can do works worthy of God's reward. The idea is both reasonable and necessary to religion. It is reasonable, because it makes all that we do depend upon the power of God, Who is Almighty; and it is a necessary idea, because without it God is false to His promises, and the practical part of religion becomes a delusion. The intelligent Catholic wonders how all this can appear otherwise to any fair-minded believer of the Bible. And in fact, for more than fifteen hundred years from the foundation of Christianity, though there may be found much variety of opinion upon the subject, and perhaps at times extreme views, there was no essential difference of authoritative teaching.

It was Luther who first strenuously opposed the idea; and from his time there may be traced a bitter prejudice at length growing into a sort of Protestant tradition which is still tenacious of life and power. Merit! The notion still strikes the "orthodox" Protestant as utterly strange, yes, abominable. Merit! You must be a Catholic or a Unitarian!—he exclaims. And here, indeed, the followers of natural and supernatural goodness can fraternize a little, to say the least.

It would take us too far afield to describe thoroughly the intricate workings of Luther's error which were so perniciously fruitful. We shall touch upon such as more directly relate to our subject. Merit is a kind of sequel or corollary to the Catholic doctrine of justification. When this man set up his heresy of justification by faith alone, boldly glorying in it as an innovation and as the article by which the Church must stand or fall, one plain inference from his teaching was that there could be no place for merit as there was none for good works. Faith, faith was everything; and even that not so much a belief in the Saviour or His redemption as a confidence, amounting to absolute assurance, that our sins are forgiven. No matter about being sure of repentance,—that didn't trouble him, strange to say; no matter how much we sinned,—and Luther's words about "sinning boldly" and about our "sham sins" were disgustingly shocking and tended to destroy even common morality; only let a man be absolutely sure his sins are forgiven, and "in a moment the affair is settled," and the justice of Christ is imputed to him; that is, he is called just, though he is not really made so. "This," says Bossuet with finely pointed sarcasm, "was the great indulgence (!) that Luther preached";[1] to be saved by your feelings was gaining heaven easily enough; and his Catholic biographer with a like irony asks, "Of what use were an indulgence [*i.e.*, a genuine one] to the possessor of such a pearl as that found by our soul-sick man?"[2]

These few words are enough to show why the theory of Protestantism can allow no such thing as merit. In the very origin of Protestantism there was no true idea of deliverance from sin, and of the importance of good works, works of holiness. On the other hand the

[1] *Variations of Protestantism*, i., p. 31.
[2] Audin's *Life of Luther*, i., p. 23.

Catholic teaching is that, when delivered from sin and brought into a state of grace, we not only can and must do such works, but that they are meritorious with God.

This teaching does not ignore faith by any means, but gives it its true place of dignity. Faith is the root, the foundation of justification, as the Council of Trent says. But it is to be remembered that a part of this very faith, without which Scripture declares we can not please God, consists in believing that He is a rewarder[1] of those who seek Him (Heb. xi. 6). Faith looks forward with hope to good works done through charity which shall be worthy of His reward. Nor is faith ever to be laid aside. It is the constant spring of action; but without this action, these good works—wrought by God's power in us, yet by our free will co-operating, and so our own—faith, as an apostle plainly tells us, would be dead, fruitless; and by these good works we are as truly justified as by the faith which prompts them.

The Bible, and particularly the New Testament, is full of the Catholic teaching of merit.

[1] The word is a strong one, meaning "a payer of wages."

Christ and His apostles are continually declaring the absolute necessity of good works; that God is not unjust to forget them; that He will judge the world in equity; that we shall receive the things done in our bodies; that we are to be hearty in our service of God, good and faithful unto the end; that thus we shall receive our reward and enter into His joy, being worthy to stand before Him, worthy to walk with Christ in white raiment, worthy of His kingdom; that the reward shall be according to our works, even trifling acts done for Him not losing their reward, and great deeds of love and endurance being sure of recompense correspondingly great. The persecuted for His sake are especially bidden to rejoice, for great is their reward in heaven. Moses is put before us as an example, because he looked unto the reward of God's people; and St. Paul, who has fought a good fight, just before his martyrdom says there is laid up for him a crown of justice, which the Lord, the just Judge, shall give him. Almost the last words of the New Testament are, "Behold, I come quickly and My reward is with Me, to render to every man according to his works."

If any imagine that Catholic teaching encourages pride or self-righteousness, because it makes so much of merit, they are grievously mistaken. The source of merit is the grace of God. "When He crowns our merits, He crowns His own gifts," as St. Augustine aptly writes. But the point is, that the just are really enabled to keep His commandments, and that they thus do merit His promised reward. Always bearing in mind both God's grace and man's free co-operation, there is nothing strange or unreasonable in the teachings of the Council of Trent, that "the just for their good works done in God ought to expect and hope for an eternal recompense from Him, through His mercy and the merit of Jesus Christ, if so be that they persevere unto the end," etc.; and that the good works of such "merit increase of grace, eternal life, . . . and also an increase of glory"; for certainly, as the same authority claims, "the glory of God and the merits of Christ are not in any way derogated from by the Catholic doctrine, but rather made illustrious."[1]

Two or three further points of interest re-

[1] Sess. vi., Can. 26, 32, 33.

lating to merit here suggest themselves. Merit may be, in a sense, lost and regained. Christianity as normally presented by the Church is not a religion of presumption. Luther's false assurance is no part of it. It teaches constant hope, which can spring only from constant watchfulness and prayer. By mortal sin we may any moment lose God's grace, and then our merits, even if not destroyed, no longer profit us till our sin is forgiven and we are again justified and restored to His favor. How benignly shines forth, in this connection, the healing sacrament of Penance!

Again, there are degrees of merit, and there will be corresponding degrees of heavenly reward. Merit, greater or less, is determined by various conditions,—the character of a good work in itself, the circumstances in which it is performed, the motive and spirit of the one who does it. In all these respects, doubtless, in the other world there will be seen to be much reversal of previous human judgment. The last shall be first and the first last. Many will be just saved and others will take high places in heaven. The reward will be as they have justly merited; and the highest attainment will be found to have flowed from the deepest humility. What wholesome introspection do we continually need, what childlike simplicity as well, whether we seek only to obey God's plain precepts, or aspire to walk in the way of Christian perfection!

Once more, this present life is the time for gaining merit, and the only time. The night of death ends the day of trial. In that night no man can work. Future probation, as it is called, has no place in Catholic teaching. Purgatory is not for that purpose, as some seem to fancy. Cleansing and further discipline, so far as needed, are for those who leave this life justified. Judgment, merciful and just, will be according as we have followed the light given us; and no one can say he has had no opportunity. Considering the uncertainty of life and the certainty of death, that the present is all we have, if the eternal reward is *now* being gained or lost, what stronger incentive can there be for effort?

The power of this true doctrine of merit as a motive must be evident from the various lights in which we have placed it. If suffering, as satisfaction for sin, can be so appealed to as was described in our last paper, what can not be said of this motive of merit, in the Christian life? That other motive was negative at best—a dreadful negative, indeed, but evil is only the absence of good—this is richly positive. That meant to prevent, to put down, to destroy, this is to gain, to achieve, to build up. That spoke of punishment, this speaks of reward. That was to escape hell, this is to enter heaven. And while the two states are strictly alternative—if we escape one we gain the other—how much better is it to keep before ourselves the glorious reward! —as much better as light is better than darkness, love than fear. The sufferings of this present life are not to be compared with the glory which shall be revealed; if we suffer for Christ we shall reign with Him; these are true views of life, we know; but no truer than that we are to labor to enter into His rest, to do good works continually, looking to the reward and more and more striving to make ourselves worthy of it.

This is the teaching of many of the Church's prayers; *e.g.*—" that we may *worthily* obtain that which Thou dost promise, make us to love that which Thou dost command";—" grant that as we venerate him [one of the saints] for our protector on earth, we may *deserve* to be aided by his intercession in heaven";—" grant that we may *deserve* to keep in mind the lessons of His [Christ's] patience, and also to be made partakers of His Resurrection";—" that we may *worthily abound in good works*";—" that we may *deserve* to obtain of Thy mercy the pardon of our sins and the *rewards* promised to the penitent"; —" that we may be found *worthy* to arrive at the light that never faileth";—" that we, being *worthy* . . . may *deserve* to be presented in the holy temple of Thy glory";— " pray for us, O holy Mother of God, that we may be *made worthy* of the promises of Christ." These and many more like petitions show the Church's devotional spirit.

To carry out this spirit in the life is what the Catholic ideal is constantly seeking to accomplish. Rightly apprehended, no other motive equals this of merit. More than any other it nerves for endurance, cheers in toil, comforts under discouragement, rouses in apparent failure, makes common, even despised duties noble, puts heroism into life, and leads to the crown of perseverance. Whether in the eye of men or in the veriest obscurity, in positions of honor or neglected and despised, we know for Whom we labor, Who gives us power, and what His grace means; and while we seek His praise and strive for His reward, it is because the praise and the reward are from Him Whom we love. It is a slander hardly worth noticing to say that gaining this reward of eternal life is a base, mercenary matter. The contrary is true. "The desire for heaven," it has been well observed, "is neither a spiritual form of selfishness nor a calculation of interests."[1] We are not God's slaves, but His sons, in the Church. It is love for Jesus, the strongest personal love, disinterested, self-sacrificing, which has always fired the Church's missionary zeal, inspired the virtues of saints, and been at the root of all genuine Christian experience in the daily lives of the faithful. Can not this love, in every sphere of action, also keep in mind the promised reward of Him Who said, "In My

[1] Aubrey De Vere's *Essays*, ii., p. 213.

Father's house are many mansions; I go to prepare a place for you "? We long to be there, with Him, forever.

Such a reward, such a heaven, thus arduously and enthusiastically labored for, is alone commensurate with the dignity of human nature made just and pure by the grace of God. Christian merit is the motive with which we appeal to the world's unrest seeking an avenue for its legitimate activity. Here, in Christian attainment, as the Catholic religion alone puts it before men, is the field for labor where energies are neither perverted nor paralyzed. That religion does not leave men under the dominion of their feelings, but would bring them into the service of the great Rewarder of good works. Here their restless powers may have fullest sweep; for the highest achievement, the grandest destiny may await them. This is no extolling of mere natural goodness, but it is a glorying in goodness made possible and certain by the grace of God. The Church does not timidly keep back the great truth of merit, speaking of it in a whisper, with fear and trembling. There is no call for that. That is not the Gospel of

Christ. Such blighting of human powers springs from the errors of Protestantism. God is not unjust. By His grace we do good works. They are really our works, for He says so. They merit His promised reward, and this they will surely receive.

XVIII

THE SAINTS, AND OUR RELATIONS TO THEM

THIS word *saint*—a holy person—may have a wide range of meaning and application. It belongs to all times. There were saints, and great saints, before the coming of Christ. It denotes various gradations of holiness. In the New Testament all worthy Christians are commonly called saints, and the use is even extended to all believers, worthy or unworthy. Naturally, in the language of the Church, *the saints* long ago came to mean particularly those eminent in holiness among the faithful—possibly kept by God's grace, as we may believe the Blessed Virgin was, entirely sinless—certainly free from all grievous sins, patterns of various graces, abounding in positive good works, standards of heroic virtue. The record of history shows that many such have been canonized, that is, their place of honor has been definitely recognized by the

Variety of Gifts in the Saints

Church's authority,[1] they are pronounced worthy of veneration by the faithful, and they are invoked at the Church's altars.

From the Blessed Virgin and the holy apostles down, what richness of attainment has there been in the saints! What variety of character, of natural and supernatural gifts! Some have led lives of constant contemplation, others of almost ceaseless action. Some have been so engrossed with the supernatural that they have seemed "to have no part in earth or in human nature"; with others the supernatural has so united with nature that they have been not the less men because they were saints. Some have been of intellect most powerful and commanding; others, divinely wise, have been as simple as untaught children.

The saints, it has been well said, always our standard, are not always our examples. Aside from their peculiarities, which have been compared with the eccentricities of genius, "their

---

[1] At first by bishops, but since the twelfth century (Alexander III.) by Popes alone. Canonization is largely, and it would appear reasonably, held to proceed from the Church's infallibility; but this is not a point of authoritative teaching.

level," as Cardinal Newman somewhere observes, "is very different from our own, and we can not understand them," and so "we may refrain from judging, without proceeding to imitate." But their heroic sanctity always appeals to us, and we are to aspire after it; for in this they are mirrors of Christ. We must know Him first that we may know them; and then by knowing them we know Him more fully Who is the King of saints.[1] The saintly ideal is very far above us; but, though we may not attain to it, that is no reason why we should not aspire. We have the perfect example of Christ Himself; shall we make no attempt to approach that? shall we despise it? Just so of the saints; and one of them, St. Paul, urges us to be followers of him, as he is of Christ (1 Cor. xi. 1),—which gives divine authority for saintly models.

But men say that the lives of so many of the saints are either impossibilities or absurdities; either lies—that they knew no such temptations and no such victories as are recorded of them, or childish nonsense—as in

[1] This thought is finely wrought out in Aubrey De Vere's essay upon St. Aloysius. *Essays*, ii., pp. 234-36.

many of their reputed miracles. Yet, reserving always the right to distinguish baseless legends from authentic history, we affirm that such criticism upon the lives of saints is of trifling worth. Can Protestantism, which, in its revolt against God's Church, from the first threw contempt upon His saints, which so largely scouts the miraculous and makes light of the sense of nearness to the spiritual world, be a just judge of what these saints were? The humility, the purity, the self-sacrifice, and many other qualities to be found in their lives cannot be questioned. Peculiarities may exist together with most exalted goodness; these are not criticized, but rather admired when genius is read of. As for miracles, they rest upon evidence. Why God should not grant miracles in answer to prayer to-day as well as in the first age of the Church can hardly be told; and why St. Gregory, or St. Francis Xavier, or St. Philip Neri should not work a miracle as well as St. Peter or St. Paul is hard to answer.

The Church's definite teaching concerning our relations to the saints has the hold which it has upon us largely because it so appeals to human sympathy. Their lives, often enveloped in mystery, were thoroughly human. Lifted up by the supernatural, they were also natural. The saints are men and women who once walked our earth, with our human nature, our human joys, sorrows, temptations. Their victories, here won by grace, were human; their merits—God's gifts—were their own, were human. They wrought out God's purpose for them to perfection; that perfection, with heaven's glory upon it, is also human. Humanity exalted by grace is the link which, since the assumption of humanity by the Son of God, binds earth to heaven in the persons of His saints.

What is that definite teaching, that upon which the Church chiefly dwells? *The communion of saints* expresses it in a word; our fellowship with them and theirs with us. We are "fellow citizens with the saints," says holy Scripture. Our Christian privilege is not only one of nearness to "the heavenly Jerusalem," and to "myriads of angels," but to "the spirits of the just made perfect" (Heb. xii. 23); and this not simply a promise, as most Protestants explain it, but a present fact.

Now the question is,—can fellowship mean blank ignorance on both sides? If not, is this communion, on our part, only cold and silent thought of them, and on their part a vague something we know not what? More than this is reasonable to be believed. The Church, directing our thoughts to the saints reigning with Christ in heaven, tells us that they there intercede for us, that we do well to ask that intercession, that we are to venerate them, and (in a lower degree) all that directly reminds us of them, their relics, statues, images.

All this, we claim, is reasonable teaching. As with other points of doctrine, we do not propose to develop its proof. The Catholic Church finds sufficient authority for it in Scripture, and abundant confirmatory evidence in tradition, from the witness of the catacombs and from the writings of the Fathers. But there are broad general principles here, and the reasonableness of their application may be brought out a little; for this science of the saints, as it may be called, learned and practised in various manners and degrees as the Church wisely permits, has been a continued source of strength to the millions of her children. This teaching rounds out the circle of Christian faith and aspiration as nothing else can. Its hearty acceptance would do much for the unrest of the world, which finds no sufficient object in any theory of the unseen that Protestantism can present, and is only being aggravated by many false pretensions.

The saints intercede for us. On Christian principles it is not natural nor reasonable to believe otherwise. Do we not pray for each other here on earth? Why should such prayer cease in the communion of saints? Have they no longer knowledge of us? There is no ground for such an idea. Has their love for us ceased? It is impossible. Both knowledge and love not only exist, but must be vastly enlarged. They no more need to pray for themselves; but they can and do pray for us, for individuals and for the Church militant and all its wants. To think differently would be to contradict principles of humanity, to deny the laws of our being. Of the value of their prayers it is enough to say that human nature owns the general worth of intercession, that it is " a first principle of the Church's life," and that its power with God is in proportion to sanctity. The saints, the near friends of God, particularly the Blessed Virgin, may

> "move the hand that moves the world,"

when our own imperfect prayers, and even "the prayer of a just man" on earth, which we know "availeth much," might come far short.

If, then, they are willing and able to help us, and prayer is their resource, why may we not ask them for this help? Indeed it is reasonable; and no fair objection can be brought against the usage. The prayer of a saint is not, says Father Hunter, "something different in kind from the prayer made by a man on earth, however much increase of efficacy results from the holiness of the saint and his union with God. . . . The Catholic who invokes a saint knows well that the person invoked can of his own power do nothing; all his power arises from the bountifulness of God; in this respect it is like the prayer of any man on earth."[1]

[1] *Dogmatic Theology*, iii., p. 469.

If the suggestions of common sense were heeded and the common humanity of saints with ourselves remembered, much of the non-Catholic feeling against asking their prayers might be seen to be foolish and might disappear. So would the notion that such usage is apt to lessen the frequency or the earnestness of our direct prayers to God, which all Catholic experience contradicts. So, certainly, would the objection that their intercession and our invocation of them takes from the glory due to Our Lord, or depreciates the infinite merit of His mediation. That mediatorship is unique, and can not thus be interfered with. That alone is essential; this of the saints is not essential, and is but the permitted and natural reaching out of human heart to human heart in the divinely appointed fellowship which brings us to God. Yet that mistaken notion of taking honor from Christ and His mediation we know has troubled many an honest soul. As earnest and sincere a Catholic convert as ever lived says of himself during his years of trial,—" It was a long time before I got over my difficulty on the score of the devotion paid to the saints," and that it was difficulty relating to their intercession we may believe from what he writes after twenty years of Catholic life: "This I know full well, . . . that the Catholic Church allows no image, material or immaterial, no dogmatic symbol, no rite, no sacrament, no saint, not even the Blessed Virgin herself, to come between the soul and its Creator. It is face to face, 'solus cum solo,' in all matters between man and his God."[1] This utterance, so strong and so true, may be recommended to all inquiring minds that have fear about human intercessors. If individuals here and there go beyond Catholic sanction in belief or practice, the Church is not responsible for their abuses.

And what is veneration? It is honor, reverence, a kind of homage, a kind of worship. Men venerate the great and good, and do homage to dignitaries. There are worshipful magistrates; and in the Anglican marriage service are the words "with my body I thee worship." Now no one pretends that the worship of saints is not more than this; but because modern and Protestant usage has

[1] Newman's *Apologia*, pp. 195, 196 (edition of 1886).

restricted the term to divine honor, it need not mean as much as that, nor does it. It is high honor, very high, and towards the Blessed Virgin the highest possible towards a creature, but even this differs both infinitely in degree and essentially in kind from the homage or worship paid to God. To render that to saints would be idolatry. We may charitably suppose that many have innocently preferred that false charge against Catholics because of the word *worship*, which with them has borne quite another meaning.

We venerate the saints, then; and this veneration is reasonable. It is " a privilege, nay a duty, and has a normal place in revealed religion."[1] To Catholics the saints are not as pagan gods; though even on this point it is to be said that Christianity has never denied the good in paganism, but has gloried in admitting it. As the living manifestation of normal Christianity, the Church has taken the impulses of polytheism and purified them. No one has more wisely expressed this than Cardinal Newman, who writes: " In proportion as the extinction of the old corrupt hea-

[1] Newman's *Via Media*, Preface to third edition, p. lxxi.

Reverence for Relics and Images

thenism made it possible, she has invoked saints, sanctioned the use of their images, and, in the spirit of the Gospels and the Acts, has expected miracles from their persons, garments, relics, and tombs."[1] But to make of the saints demigods, and of their veneration "a new mythology," a pagan idolatry,—this, so far from being true of the Church, is the very opposite of what she has done. The veneration which she enjoins, as has been often pointed out, is the Christian's great safeguard against the revival of such idolatry, in some worship of nature, of heroes, or of self.[2]

There is nothing in the lower, relative veneration encouraged by the Church towards relics and images of the saints which ought to be objected to by fair-minded people. Reverence for relics is a principle inherent in human nature. Individuals, societies, communities, governments manifest it towards whatever has belonged to the great and illustrious,—dwellings, furniture, garments, even towards little insignificant things, only because they once owned them. The world has protected

[1] Preface to *Via Media*, p. lxxiv.
[2] See Aubrey De Vere's *Essays*, ii., p. 252, etc.

their dead bodies from desecration, and has honored their graves with costly tombs. What wonder if the Church teach that the holy bodies of martyrs and saints are to be venerated by the faithful?—if she place their relics in her altars, or enclose them in magnificent shrines? Further, the living bodies of apostles, we know from Scripture, possessed miraculous powers; what wonder if even the lifeless bodies or the bones of other saints should have had like virtues? The veneration in any case is shown to the relics only relatively. The saints themselves are honored, and the honor redounds to God, Who works miracles, answers prayers, or quickens faith and love.

Images, statues, or pictures of saints are venerated upon a similar principle of reasonableness. They are meant to remind of those whom they represent; "not," says the Council of Trent, "that any divinity or virtue is believed to be in them, . . . or that anything is to be asked of them, or that trust is to be reposed in images, . . . but the honor which is shown them is referred to the prototypes which those images represent."

While much more might be said upon this whole topic, it really seems unnecessary. The substance of the Catholic teaching is in these few words. Portraits or statues in churches are not invoked nor adored. Catholics are not worshipers of idols. These material symbols, differently to different minds, help thought and incite devotion. Sometimes, like relics, they are means for exhibiting miraculous power. They are intended to honor the saints; and rightly reminding of the saints they bring devout worshipers to God.

XIX

PERSONAL OBSTACLES,—THOSE WHICH CATHOLICS MIGHT REMOVE

HAVING now considered the chief distinctive points of Catholic doctrine and usage, and shown their reasonableness as far as possible, perhaps, in so brief a space, we turn attention to various hindrances of a personal nature which must be noticed before these papers are brought to a close.

As was stated at the entrance upon our subject, the weakness and wilfulness of human nature and the observed imperfections of Christianity are enough to account for the force of all obstacles to the Catholic religion, and to make it plain why men continue to reject that divine institution, the Church, the acceptance of which can alone quiet the fever of their unrest or direct its rightful aim. Stumbling blocks in the path of an inquiring non-Catholic, then, as would be supposed, may relate to something besides beliefs and doctrines and usages of the Church. After all these have been explained, there remains the personal element, which often presents a mightier obstacle than all theoretical difficulties of Catholic teaching put together. Here is a practical matter. Those who hold the doctrines and practise the usages, priests or people, are they not imperfect, it may be said,—many of them exceedingly so? Those, too, who are inquiring into the Church's claims, with much sincerity examining, considering, deciding, are they not very human, yes, again and again very weak or wilful?

It shall be our aim to be fair to both these classes; and while treating of personal topics to avoid all "personality." But to say nothing at this juncture is plainly impossible, either in justice to our subject or to meet honestly the question which prompted the writing of these papers—a question put by one of our most zealous and influential priests—"Why do not more Protestants, here among us, come into the Catholic Church?" There are various reasons why they do not; some, as has been seen, springing from ignorance and inherited prejudice, perhaps from failure to understand what the Church really teaches, but some reasons also personal to those who profess the Catholic faith, and certainly many in inquirers themselves. In a word—to quote a saying of another wise priest—" What keeps non-Catholics from entering the Church is what keeps Catholics from living up to it."

As regards the hindrances which Catholics, with more or less of fault, may present, it goes without saying that no one of them touches the nature or character of the Church itself. Even if we were to consider the moral failings sometimes charged against her ministers, which we shall not, any charge which might possibly be brought could take nothing in the least from the sacredness of the priestly office, or from the necessity and validity of its ministrations. Many Protestants do seem so eager to catch at every instance of moral delinquency in this quarter!—a proof, in itself, of the exalted character which is generally expected and as generally maintained. It would be hardly possible that there should be no unworthy, even immoral Catholic clergymen,—for they are human; but how few there are! Moreover, the lives of the clergy are exposed to peculiar temptations which only the special grace of God can enable them to meet. St. Paul in writing to the Corinthians (II. Cor. iv. 7) refers to " the treasure in earthen vessels"; and when we weigh all the facts we may well wonder at the immense preponderating influence of consistent example and eminent holiness which we see, rather than cavil at the comparatively few defections from the high ideal of the priesthood. No more shall here be said upon this topic; but there are one or two other objectionable points, even in those who are the Church's authorized guides and teachers, which may be respectfully alluded to. In so doing we are not constituting ourselves critics of those who are above us; we are only uttering, in the Church's truest interest, the common sentiment of a great many people, the faithful within, well-wishers and would-be-Catholics without. Until perfection is reached in anything, reform is always in order; and purity of motive ought to be sufficient protection against misunderstanding.

For one thing, then, the preaching in most

Catholic churches might be greatly improved. The priest, we do not forget, is the official ambassador of Christ; and his preaching proclaims the word of God. But it is a mistake to presume upon this prerogative, as some seem to do. There is a wide distinction between the word of God and the weak utterances of many men; and the hearers of sermons, even in the most uneducated congregation, have more power of thinking than they are sometimes credited with. Too often Catholic preaching is not strong, but exceedingly weak, with little if any clear exposition of truth or weighty enforcing of precept. It is not enough to be able to point to many thoughtful and forcible preachers, in both city and country, yes, to several justly noted as pulpit-orators. What is still to be desired is a vastly greater number of those whose preaching shows any considerable breadth of knowledge, vigor and balance of thought, and aptness of expression, together with a fair ability in speaking as well as in writing. At present there is too much of the very opposite of all this. The general standard needs to be raised. Our Catholic preaching (for to this country alone these remarks refer) ought to range far above the level of a respectable mediocrity.

It is not for us to enlarge upon this defect, nor is this the place for suggesting to what such a condition of things may be due. The causes are various. Let every palliation by way of existing circumstances be brought forward, for there is much good excuse. The fact is evident; and just as fast as the evil is remedied—for it must be and will be, more and more—the Church will appear in her true light, that of a wise adaptation to the needs of this land and this age, possessing an effective means for edifying the faithful and for winning back wanderers to the True Fold which, here and now, it must be owned, she too much lacks.[1]

---

[1] In addition to the book referred to on the next page, much food for thought and much valuable information concerning the present needs and the present and prospective opportunities and attainments of our Catholic theological students may be found in a paper upon "Our American Seminaries," by the Rt. Rev. B. J. McQuaid, D.D., Bishop of Rochester, published in *The American Ecclesiastical Review* for May, 1897. And, since the conditions of the question go back to previous education, all interested should read the strong article by the Rev. John T. Murphy, C.S.Sp., in *The Ameri-*

In presuming to allude to the perfunctory way of many clergymen in official ministrations we but call attention to a fault condemned by highest authorities and continually deplored, yet strangely keeping its hold, doing great harm to Catholics, and preventing many Protestants from ever becoming Catholics. This perfunctoriness—to use a mild term—has many phases; we touch upon but one, its most trying manifestation, which is in the most sacred of all the Church's services, that of the Mass. A recent Catholic writer, himself a priest, with rebuke none too sharp tells of " the curious spectacle of good priests officiating at the public prayers of the Church in the rapid, offhand style peculiar to handlers of red tape."[1] The heart of every devout Catholic must respond to his criticism of the

can Catholic Quarterly Review for July, 1897, upon " Catholic Secondary Education in the United States." It is in harmony with the spirit of such men—progressive educators as well as high ecclesiastics they may reverently be called— that the author would be considered as making the statements which he does in this paper.

[1] Rev. John Talbot Smith's *The Training of a Priest*, p. 180, etc. This is the second edition of a book first published in 1896, with the title *Our Seminaries*.

"astonishing rapidity," the "trolley speed" with which the Mass is often said, and of the treatment which the Holy Sacrifice thus receives through the apparent thoughtlessness of those who must be in heart most highly honoring it and intending to inculcate this honor in the people.

The philosophy of this so common practice is to be found, we imagine, only in a growing custom of haste. We live in a hurrying age, and perhaps Americans are unusually apt to make a business of the public duties of their religion. At all events, here is a habit, a way of one and another, but, of however many, a way independent of all training. The writer just quoted must know his ground when he says that those who so err have "no excuse for lack of reverence to the Holy Sacrifice"; for no seminary has ever failed "to impress its students with the awful dignity of the Mass, and the absolute necessity of decency and propriety in all the details of the Sacrifice."

The explanation, occasionally ventured, that all this is an action which hastens to its climax, does not satisfy; the extreme speed which is practised can be called only an abuse of both attention and intention. Words are the medium of thought; and if there is any significance in the use of spoken words, it must be all lost and worse than lost if words become an utter jumble. The mind of the utterer must be left blank by such use; while the minds of worshiping hearers are thrown into confusion, in which it is not strange if grief is mingled with indignation, until the hardening force of habit blunts the sensibilities or the known sacredness of what is being done restores mental and spiritual equilibrium. If it be said that the hearers are not regarded as such—that they are worshipers, for whom an offering is being made to God—it may fairly be answered that all approach to God with words of worship must have limits of outward reverence, and that *worshipers* among the people can not help being *listeners* to the words of the offering priest, and can not divest themselves (and ought not) of the principles of reverence and of common sense. Much more might be said upon this topic; but we refrain. We have been careful to allege no moral failing, no culpable inattention. If such ever exists, it is not for us to judge it. We are thinking of what is actually seen and heard—of the unquestionable impression; and with all respect we ask,—Is it not time that many put a check upon their breathless haste? Because of the deep conviction, yes, the certain knowledge that here is a grave stumbling block to non-Catholics, and one which can and ought to be removed, we speak our honest opinion.

Coming now to general matters, it may be said that an improvement in the spirit of Catholic journalism must be looked for, if the Church's superior excellence is to be made known in this way to the world without. The field for comment is here very wide;[1] but our words shall be few and general. To begin with a note of commendation,--all honor to those who are striving, against whatever discouragements, to elevate Catholic journalism! Catholic papers may be the greatest help or the greatest hindrance to the Catholic cause.

[1] We speak only of our own country, and of nothing beyond daily and weekly papers. The number of these, according to Hoffmann's *Catholic Directory* for 1898, is 162, published in nine different languages, 94 of them in English.

The Holy Father has often called attention to their influence, with words of praise and of warning. They should be able, clean, dignified, high-toned. They should be instructive in morals and religion, with variety in the subjects presented and an interesting way of treating them. Not all these qualities, perhaps, can be everywhere sufficiently commanded. Business talent as well as literary is needed, and pecuniary resources are essential for pecuniary success.

But are all American Catholic journals what they might be?—is the question. We do not say—are they all able? for this could not be, any more than in any other kind of journalism; but have all of them the other qualities we have mentioned? Are they all estimable? —perhaps we might say, respectable? Is there not narrowness almost verging upon bigotry, too much bitterness, personal aggressiveness, petty sarcasm, flippant smartness admitted to the columns of many of them? Some seem to affect the sensational style of certain secular papers; others say unjust things about non-Catholics, or improve every chance for a mean fling, forgetting that such uncharitableness is no part of fair controversy, and that it generally reacts upon ourselves in stifling the spirit of inquiry into Catholic claims. We make no comparisons, among ourselves or with others. Whatever papers, Catholic or Protestant, may indulge in this sort of talk, it is no justification for us. If we realize our obligation to use as best we may that most valuable ally, the power of the press, we shall see that there is much room for improvement in this matter of journalism. Positive, charity-inspired teaching, always courteous, always high-toned, by this silent means widespread, will do far more for Catholic truth than all the pugnacity and boastfulness which from time to time have prevailed.

These last two qualities, we regret to say, are much too common among Catholics in every walk of life. In public assemblies, in social gatherings, with how many does "fight or boast" seem to be the motto which they persistently flaunt, especially where the Church is concerned! But is not such an attitude quite uncalled for? If we are sure of our position—as we have every reason to be—we can well dispense with a little of this spirit.

We haven't yet won America to Catholicity, nor, we submit, is this the way to win it. Protestantism is not yet dead, by any means, in spite of the complacent assurance to be noted here and there, and even occasionally the strange addition of the Church's blessing, *requiescat in pace!*

Moreover, in their anxious defence of authority, are not some Catholics a little too afraid of the spirit of progress? A true liberality, a candid broad-mindedness is not inconsistent with a strong, uncompromising hold upon Catholic principles and an earnest advocacy of them. Liberalism in religion, as generally understood among us, is to be condemned; but it is only a fallacy, a gross misuse of terms, that a Catholic who is liberal should be sometimes scouted as an anomaly, a contradiction. We can not thus dispose of the school of thought and opinion—if any choose to call it so—which contains some of the grandest names in the Church; and we thus utterly misrepresent the truly broadest religion in the world, and turn back multitudes who are waiting at its doors!

This kind of stricture upon Catholics by

Catholics, so unedifying, suggests the general remark that there might well be among us a stronger manifestation of the spirit of love and harmony. Human nature is human nature, we know; Christianity does not at once transform that nature, but gradually moulds and shapes it. Yet the divine principle is always at work, and in nothing more emphatically than in securing obedience to that " new commandment " of love which our Lord gave to His disciples. Aside from the direct benefits which this love confers, its witness to the world is not to be lost sight of. He Himself said,—" By this shall all men know that you are My disciples, if ye have love one for another." The glorious ideal of unity which the Church holds up is sadly dimmed, if not practically lost to the world just so far as the opposite spirit prevails. Unity of faith and worship is not, for it can not be, thereby contravened; but certainly it is not bearing the fruit which it should, in proving itself to be " the unity of the Spirit in the bond of peace " (Eph. iv. 3).

Now the opposite temper has been seen to break out all too often among Catholics, and those perhaps of the most orthodox. Indeed priests as well as people might furnish many instances, sometimes of a spirit of envious ambition, sometimes of keen rivalry, sometimes of severe depreciation or cold indifference. All such dispositions, wherever manifested, are not, it must be owned, convincing arguments to the non-Catholic mind for the love which should flow from the one faith. To look at another point,—here in our wide country the different elements of its population are being gradually blended by a community of interest. Should not a force at least as strong be found in the Catholic faith? Why among different races and nationalities of Catholics must there still be jealousies, and in certain sections, as inquiry shows, bitterly active? "The divisions, hostilities and misunderstandings which now prevail in sections where priests and people of different nationalities live and mingle" have caused a recent writer to complain that "the faith seems to throw Catholics of different races farther apart."[1] Allowing for possible mistakes in this testimony or exaggerations in this lan-

[1] *The Training of a Priest*, ut. sup., p. 264.

guage, any such state of things must form a mighty obstacle to the spread of the Catholic religion, and should more and more be done away. Men can not be blamed for saying " by their fruits ye shall know them "; and while perfection in this regard is not to be expected, there is reason to look for a much nearer approach to the condition which called out the exclamation, in the Church's early days,—" See, how these Christians love one another!"[1]

We have not chosen to bring forward in this paper the personal hindrances which belong under the head of open immorality or wickedness in professing Catholics high or low. There is no need of it. Such cases speak for themselves. Vaunting hypocrites, open dissemblers are found among the false followers of all religions. The common sense of mankind is not long disturbed by them, but takes them for what they are worth.

[1] The International Catholic Congress, the fourth session of which was held in 1897, at Freiburg, Switzerland, where seven hundred members were present, and papers were read in Latin, English, French, German and Italian, is doing a good work in securing a harmony of sentiment and friendly relations between Catholics of different nationalities.

And so of the grossly wicked. So far as such are found among us, they are only nominal Catholics. Perhaps some would claim that more should be done than is done to reclaim them; but the Church can not perform impossibilities, and whoever is well informed must admit that many wise and efficient methods, and in most faithful hands, are now in operation in their behalf.

XX

PERSONAL OBSTACLES,—THOSE FOR WHICH INQUIRERS ARE RESPONSIBLE

THOSE who are examining the claims of the Catholic religion may themselves, directly or indirectly, put most weighty obstacles in the way of their accepting it. Full, intelligent consent is what is required. But various excuses, apparently more or less legitimate, may arise, and consent may be withheld or delayed. Who can say that, if all outward circumstances were favorable, and then if inquirers always heeded their reason and obeyed their conscience, there would not be at once and continuously such a return of wanderers to the fold, such an influx into the One, Holy, Catholic Church as has not been known since its earliest days? This is what enthusiastic Catholics can not help believing; and what, if some sort of spiritual Roentgen rays could be turned upon the interior life of thousands in their unrest, we are confident they themselves could not help admitting. Except by miracle, it cannot be presumed there will ever be such a Pentecostal return. Human nature is not likely to meet the conditions. Certainly in our time we must be content to see the Church grow, so far as it grows from without, by individual conversions, while we have to be thankful for the large numbers who are thus coming one by one.

It is well to look at some of the hindrances which stand in the way of inquirers, from themselves or their circumstances; for what those who are religiously disturbed—as so many are—must do if they would please God and be sure of His peace, is to use their reason, to follow conscience, to submit their will; in short, to conquer themselves, and, as God's Providence shows them the way, to conquer circumstances.

Oh, these personal circumstances, which so invest, which may so perplex, harass, dismay, when the great question of one's life, the change of religion, demands definite answer! Here is often to be found most serious hindrance to both duty and desire. No one who has not known it can estimate the pressure. The difficulty takes many forms. A practical one relates to occupation and pecuniary support. A man who has no family ties may not be brought into trouble on this score; but he who has " given hostages to fortune " can not think lightly of occupation and income taken away, and of not knowing what can be done for the support of those who are dependent upon him and to whom he has plainest obligations. The hardest trials of this kind naturally come upon Protestant ministers with families. By the rule of celibacy they can not become priests; and at present there are but few lines of occupation open to Catholic educated laymen, as such. This matter of a livelihood has delayed or finally stopped many a man morally convinced of Catholic truth. Duty to others in temporal things has seemed so to conflict with duty to self (and to others?) in things spiritual, that action has been paralyzed. To speak at all fully of such cases is not possible here. It would be very easy to give a harsh judgment which might be unjust. We only venture to say that often the true course to conquer circumstances, is *to act*, with generous, implicit trust in God's Providence, and that the way is often wonderfully opened to the use of all right means, with courage and perseverance.

A trying circumstance which not a few have to meet is the loss of social position. This, too, it is difficult to speak of properly here. But it may fairly be asked—what any one changes one's religion for. Is it a question of social status one way or the other? If so, the depth or the sincerity of conviction may well be doubted. It is the honor of the Catholic Church everywhere to be the Church of the poor. In our own country, except in a few large cities, the Catholic people still belong generally to the laboring class. If the convert can keep former non-Catholic friendships without compromising principle, why not? If this can not be, the cross, such as it is, surely ought cheerfully to be borne. What is it, compared with many that might be named? Worth will ultimately find its level; and the companionable will not be left without companionship.

A severer trial from without is this. In spite of increasing broad-mindedness as the Catholic

Church has come to be better understood in the community, it is pitiful that coldness, opposition, alienation, even persecution from friends and kindred against one who wishes to become a Catholic are still not unknown, and are forces brought directly to bear. Many times, if the wished-for change is carried out, the screws are tightened rather than loosened. In some families still—and made up of sincere Christian people (!)—it is a fact that one might better become anything else, Deist, Buddhist, or Agnostic, to keep peace with those of his own flesh and blood! Are there no Catholics who in becoming Catholics have lost for the rest of life the love of father or mother, brother or sister? Are there none who have been disinherited?—who have given up large fortunes? The true answer to these questions might surprise a great many easygoing people. Such sacrifices, such sundering of heart-strings are among the severest trials of faith in our day. Those who have to meet them need the fullest grants of God's grace, to enable them to be at the same time strong, patient, forbearing, forgiving. But all who are so situated can take but one course—that of *quiet firmness*, either for their own inward peace or for the good of all concerned. Even if they must forsake all to follow Christ, is not that what the Master bids His disciples be ready for? Have they not the comfort and support of His precious promise to those who are so called? (St. Matt. xix. 29.)

Adverse circumstances of whatever kind must in some way be overcome. In any great undertaking in life it is most true that if we do not conquer them they will conquer us. Yet this does not forbid, but all the more calls for the exercise of that judgment which is supposed to be part of man's natural endowment. We are not questioning the supreme importance of the higher, divine wisdom to guide inquirers, for which they should unceasingly pray. But it is surprising how little ordinary tact some people do show in matters of religion,—how many blunders, complications, even alienations might be avoided by a moderate use of common sense. Prejudice might often be disarmed, opposition pacified, and even favorable inclinations produced and strengthened. Rash impulsiveness does not make a hero; but calm determination which takes in the whole environment and then wisely acts may win the way for truth, and perhaps by good example lead others to it also.

The main hindrance to inquirers is in themselves. Those who are satisfied where they are we do not call inquirers, much as the Catholic religion would meet their deepest need. Unless they are disturbed—in some appreciable degree of unrest—they are not inquirers. Perhaps such might be called sleepers, or dreamers, or quiet or admiring observers, as regards the one true religion; or in other moods they are bold, bigoted opposers, bitter haters and denouncers of that religion. With all these we have now nothing to do but to commend them to God's mercy, and pray that He would open their eyes or soften their hearts. It is not for us to judge others. If they follow the light which they have, sincerely striving to know and do God's will, even in conscientious opposition to His Church, we would not deny them salvation through invincible ignorance. Of the real worth of that plea God alone can be the judge; we only affirm that it is a dangerous weapon to use in self-defence, and—sadly we say it—unquestionably many must find it so at the last.

But genuine, honest inquirers—we repeat—find, after all, the chief hindrance in themselves. Are they morally convinced of the truth of the Catholic religion? If not, may they not become so? Let them look fully into the grounds of its claims, with earnest prayer for that divine illumination without which our sin-darkened mind has no clear vision into spiritual things. Let them examine whether these claims are not proved by Holy Scripture, and by the witness of history fairly interpreted. Let them note the reasonableness of doctrine and practice as we have sketched it in these papers; and say whether the logical needs of the mind and the emotional needs of the heart are not met. Let them not make too much of those personal obstacles which Catholics present. All the failings of individuals do not weaken the argument of the grand whole. All the imperfections of the human element in the Church can not touch its integrity as a divine institution. The reasonable man will not be deterred by any facts which can be brought forward, but will go on with his inquiry.

Such investigation should be as thorough as it is honest. To it no limit of time can be set. "The Spirit breatheth where He willeth"; to His divine influence the soul of man, always free, may quickly or slowly respond. The religion of Christ is for all people. To the uneducated some one aspect of it may offer a sure hope, an unanswerable argument, and they are at once convinced; with thinking minds the study may be for months, or years. We know how it was with such eminent converts as Newman, and Manning, and Wilberforce, and Allies, and Brownson, and Hecker, and others. But superficiality in religion is always to be deprecated. How many there are who have begun such an inquiry and, after a little, coming upon some prejudice or some seeming inconsistency, or weighing possible difficulties and perhaps imagining strange terrors, have—as one described it—shut the mind with a snap, never more to open it! It is easy to see how far this is from being "invincible ignorance." It is invincible wilfulness! Let one who begins the examination of the

Catholic religion finish the work; and this is good counsel, for then no other course can possibly please God or satisfy the inquirer.

Supposing such inquiry to result in convincing—not merely of something beautiful and excellent, nor even of something to be immensely preferred—but that here is the one true revelation of God in Christ, the one normal, legitimate, full form and spirit of Christianity, why do not honest inquirers act upon their conviction? Alas! many go as far as this and no farther. Having reached this point they gradually let the subject drop from their minds. False advisers threaten or entreat; worldly cares or pleasures displace it. Now they must be occupied; now they are desperately busy; perhaps they devour novels, or go on journeys. They can not consider this matter any more, they say; and, indeed, it is not consideration which is any more needed, but action, calm, courageous, prayerful action. Refusing this, they may fancy it all remains an undecided question, and this dream may delude them for the rest of their lives; but Jesus Christ, Who once said, "He that is not with Me is against Me," knows otherwise, and that, morally convinced, they actually decided against their reason, against their conscience. Who can pretend to determine the various motives of these would-be honest inquirers? Nature and temperament, propriety and expediency come in; certainly pride as well as principle, self-esteem and human respect as truly as unselfishness and the welfare of others; all the armory of the subtle human heart seems drawn upon to defend one's course; and while weakness is so often the excuse for hesitation and inaction, the root of the trouble may be in a wilfulness which has grown more and more strong and stubborn.

For in such cases as we are describing the will is too often the seat of the difficulty. Too many people are like those obdurate Jews to whom Our Lord said, " Ye will not come to Me that ye may have life." This guiding power of the interior nature must act, must decide. When reason has spoken, and conscience has spoken, the will must assent. The essence of faith is in this entire submission of the will; and even if there has been a degree of faith before, why may there not be now a new and fuller faith, in response to God's new revelation of

Catholic truth in its fulness? One may not really be convinced, to be sure, though to the eye of man it may appear so; but we are supposing this point to have been reached. Until or unless this is the fact, let no human power sternly judge the inquirer. Certainly the Catholic Church does not. Her tenderness and gentleness, in these critical moments, may sometimes seem to the storm-tossed soul almost indifference. But what can be done, when the truth has with all fair urgency been again and again presented to one professing to seek truth? The decision, to accept or reject, must be with the inquirer. On him must rest the responsibility of choice. All the power of God's omnipotence will not take away that freedom, nor coerce the will. What can be done for the inquirer but to pray, and bid him pray for further light? Yes, and that he may not sin against light! That is the dread alternative which is so perilous. In weakness or wilfulness, from subtle pride or human respect, from expediency or some form of self-seeking to shut the mind to reason, to silence conscience, to keep back the will's assent,—this can be only sinning against light, refusing deliberately to obey the word which in repeated revelations God is speaking to the soul. How many a one, as Thomas à Kempis reminds us, needs to take good heed " lest the word which he has heard and not obeyed, known and not loved, believed and not kept, rise up in judgment against him!"

XXI

SCOPE OF THE SUBJECT—CERTAINTY AND REALITY ONLY IN THE CATHOLIC RELIGION—THE RETURN TO CHRIST

IN concluding these papers it may not be amiss to revert a little to the dignity and comprehensiveness of the subject, however imperfect may have been our way of treating it. The unrest which is in the world we have made rather a matter of frequent allusion than of direct consideration. Our thoughts have been more, we own, upon the remedy proposed; the trouble which it was to meet appearing from point to point as we have proceeded.

But how far-reaching is it all! The world's unrest! In one view it is the world's sin always seeking indulgence, or suffering from guilt, or agonizing with remorse. "The wicked are like the troubled sea that can not rest"—is the inspired picture of much human activity. In another view it is the aspiration for progress which belongs legitimately to men as creatures of God endowed with high powers, but who need and must have the guiding principle of religion. Narrowing the view somewhat, it is the longing for peace of many who may be sincerely striving to serve God, but who, biassed by imperfect knowledge of the truth, by inherited prejudice, and by many surrounding influences, are confused in thought and uncertain in action. Evidently enough they are dissatisfied with their present relations to religion; perhaps they have heard of a Church which claims to speak with genuine authority, and they are disquieted; perhaps God has given them a glimpse of truth, —they

> ". . . have seen the city, and one such glance
> No darkness can obscure," [1]

and they can not be content to wander again in the gloom. Outwardly these many people may be calm; but in their inner life they are bewildered, they know not which way to turn.

[1] Browning's "Paracelsus."

Throughout the range of civilization, whether Christian so-called or not, along with the advantages of education, the power of wealth, the appliances for comfort—or in spite of all these—runs this unrest in some form, like an under-current in the stream of life, or like a refrain in music, sad, pathetic, tragic, continually recurring, telling unmistakably the meaning of what the poet calls " the cry of the human." Instead of ceasing or growing less, it seems to increase. In the needs of the poor and ignorant, in the anxiety of the rich and the ambition of the learned, it is more and more a mark of our time. Much of our journalism, secular or religious, finds here its theme; social and civil questions in discussion make this their burden; it is the spirit continually bursting out, like the flames of a smothered fire, even in our literature. Such a spirit, such a force, may truly be called pervading in the human interests of to-day, one to be reckoned with, demanding consideration, and on reasonable ground sure to receive it if there is any such thing as a solution of its ever-insisting problem.

And the remedy! To say that God has

provided none would be to say that the problem can not be solved, that the spirit of all ages and emphatically of this age must cry out in vain for guidance and rest and peace. Such an idea is foreign to all worthy conceptions of God, and can not be entertained for a moment. There is a remedy. It proceeds from the power of God and is adapted to the nature of man. It is in the highest sense natural, yet it is far beyond nature. Its greatness, its width of reach, is amply commensurate with the deep, wide-spreading need which it is meant to satisfy. Statements like these would be admitted by all who recognize the divine origin and mission of Christianity. They may be called mere truisms. But what we affirm is that their full meaning is realized only in the Catholic religion; in other words, that here is found the one legitimate, consistent, and undeniable expression of historic Christianity. We have not attempted any detailed proof of this claim. We have presented the divine marks of the Church, and have made some suggestions as to the reasonableness of her doctrines and usages. We have tried to help the inquiring by inciting to further inquiry, persuaded that full and honest investigation, in a spirit of childlike submission to God's will, can bring, by His grace, but one result.

But we would not be misunderstood. Suppose this result—of acceptance of the true faith—were accomplished, as would it might be, in the multitudes of the Protestant world who are disquieted and confused, would there be at once a cessation of their unrest? This would be expecting too much,—more than Christianity ever promised to those who should become its disciples. There would be a radically new departure, new first principles, and these would begin to bear fruit in the heart and life. There would be faith, which shuts out doubt; the home of true unity would be seen to have been reached; the infallible Church with its infallible head would be felt to be the only sure alternative to the world's unbelief; sin would be known to be pardoned through confession, and might be more and more overcome; the Presence of Christ in the Eucharist would bring comfort and strength; merit—from Christ's own merits—would give strong incentive to effort and offer a fair field and worthy aim for all noble powers; there would be a new sense of communion with saints and angels, and an appreciation, such as no words can utter, of their blessed help, their sympathy and intercession. But, proceeding from faith—a divine gift, which reason leads up to but can not produce—all this state of things would be a gradual growth, dependent upon the individual, upon each one's use of God's grace and improvement of opportunities.

Objectors may have said throughout the course of these papers that we were trying to prove too much,—that Catholics do not show this freedom from unrest any more than Protestants. So far as Catholics are imperfect this is to be admitted. Human nature is the same in Catholic and Protestant,—a fact too often forgotten. But Catholics have a hold upon certain great principles, of authority and of freedom and of these in their mutual relations —principles which Protestants, as such, do not admit or positively reject—which give true direction to life's activities, and tend to bring to all its strivings peace. So far as they live up to their religion, Catholics gain an immunity, day by day, from unrest, which Protestants who live up to their religion can not know, for the guiding principles are not theirs. Only too much must not be expected at once. There are doubtless saints in the world now as in any past age; but the majority of good Catholic Christians, how far are they, with their faults and sins and the trials that beset them, from meeting the conditions which would ensure *no unrest!* The perfect peace of victory over evil can come only in the future life; the longing for God can be satisfied only in the Beatific Vision. When Cardinal Manning was asked by one of his old Anglican friends soon after he became a Catholic what he had found which he did not previously possess, his answer was,—"Certainty and reality." These are the paramount needs of the soul in a religion. How entirely they are met in the Catholic religion, candid examination of its origin, nature, and workings in the world may prove, and abundant experience testifies; and herein is found the sure, because divine, foundation for all the peace that is possible in this life and for perfect peace hereafter.

The opposite condition is becoming increasingly manifest throughout the Protestant world. Where are the certainty and reality? There is far less of even a semblance of these than when Manning gave his terse reply. This is true in the communion which he left to enter the Catholic Church, and it is overwhelmingly true in other Protestant bodies. Everywhere we see liberalism urging to farther advance, or the "pessimism and gloomy foreboding" of thoughtful minds, or hardened indifference with its tone of despair. All these manifestations, in however different ways, tell of present unreality and uncertainty, of change dreaded or desired. "Liberalism must be uncompromisingly bold," we read. "Aggressiveness is needed in the centres of liberal thought for the sake of the liberal forces scattered throughout the land."[1] "Americans," says a well known Unitarian,[2] "are prepared for a free religion, and our work is to arouse them to a new hope and

---

[1] These utterances are from an Episcopalian paper, called *The Church*.

[2] Rev. S. M. Crothers, in *Boston Transcript*, May 26, 1897.

courage." Another, more distinguished,[1] forgets his wonted gentleness and exclaims, "Our business is to tear away all the rags of ritual and dogma, to teach each child of God to commune with God." What certainty or reality is there in all this? The religion of nature pure and simple is made the only hope, and Church and Christianity must be destroyed! "We are coming," says still another, regarded as a leader of thought in America,[2] "to see the difference between truths and the truth, and to perceive that none of us possess the truth, and that our neighbor possesses some fragment of truth which we ourselves have failed to possess." But the Catholic faith is the truth in religion, and the Church possesses it; so Catholics may ask to be omitted from the sweep of this writer's comprehensiveness. No one has a perfect apprehension of truth; it is not possible to finite powers; but that the truth, fixed and unchangeable, was divinely revealed to

---

[1] Rev. Edward Everett Hale, D.D., at Saratoga, September, 1897.

[2] Rev. Lyman Abbott, D.D., in *The Forum*, August, 1897, p. 655.

the Church in the deposit of the faith committed to the apostles, this has always been a point of Catholic teaching. Nor is such a revelation inconsistent with a genuine development, as has been frequently explained in these pages.[1] If Doctor Abbott or his followers have only "fragments of truth," we can not but wish that they would exchange "truths" for "the truth," and possess the whole. But again, here is the uncertainty and unreality of Protestantism!

As one phase of this uncertainty especially interesting, it may be stated that the eminent Protestant theologian, Professor Harnack, of Berlin, sees in various modern manifestations "the progressive Catholicization of Protestantism." He thinks the Protestantism of the nineteenth century is being transformed, and that "this Catholicizing tendency is the chief cause of it."[2] What to him is a matter of anxious concern may be to all Catholic Christendom one of thankful rejoicing. Not that we would see a Catholicized Protestantism; there are too many now who, imbibing certain

[1] See pp. 33, 34, 41, 84, 85, 128-130.
[2] See article in *The Independent*, Dec. 24, 1896.

Catholic ideas—some of those " fragments of truth "—about doctrine, worship or usage, fancy themselves Catholics, while they cling to their Protestantism and continue in disobedience to the Church; but a general transformation of opinion such as appears to be now quietly diffusing itself may be a hopeful indication of a return to Catholic obedience and to the only divine unity. Certainly Catholics—clergy and people—are in the main responsible, under God's Providence, for hastening that result, each according to his range of influence, by spreading Catholic truth, by wisely advancing its claims, and, above all else, by exerting the power of example, the silent influence of a worthy life.

If, as is sometimes complained, Protestants know nothing of the religious life of Catholics, so far as that implies any cold exclusiveness of the latter, it is not as it should be. But such isolation is wont to be mutual. Why may they not know, if they care to? Good Catholics don't carry their religion about on their sleeve, for display or mere publicity; but daily life is permeated with its motives and purposes. It is not a secularizing of the spiritual, but a spiritualizing of what is secular; the supernatural becomes, as it were, natural, and life is lived with the spiritual world continually kept in mind and believed to be near, and the sanctions and warnings and blessings of eternity always in view. Whatever is peculiar about the Catholic religious life may be readily found out from books of devotion or from services in churches. There may be much not at once grasped by the non-Catholic mind—that should be expected by those whose belief and worship are so largely a departure from the ancient ways —but books are open, churches are open, and unprejudiced inquiry may be richly repaid.

Surely no one may think to build upon this affected ignorance, as a prominent Episcopalian clergyman did a while ago, the conceit of ignoring the Catholic Church. And he is speaking of what he calls "the Church of America,"—of the religious life of the American people! "The Church of Rome," he says, "lies so far outside the church-life of this country, or, I should say, perhaps, the Protestant life, that it need not be discussed" (!) . . . "I think it well to leave out this great branch (!) of Roman Catholicism altogether, simply because *it is so little influenced by, and has so little influence upon, the religious life of the American people*" (!)[1] This is cutting the Gordian knot, indeed! It has been often one way of solving problems which present insuperable difficulties. But the cool assumption here can only provoke ridicule in any fair-minded person; and as for the religious life of the American people, everybody must know how widely that is Catholic already. The future can be safely predicted to show no less influence; and, let us hope, for the good of those who are now so ignorant of Catholic life, that it will be far more. Evidently, as this writer affirms, " the people are restless, dissatisfied, uneasy." But the inference—" this discontent is our opportunity "—does not follow with much meaning for a communion so vague, uncertain, compromising, contradictory as that which he represents. Even " the leadership of Protestantism," to which some of these Episcopalian friends aspire, would be indignantly scorned

[1] Rev. S. D. McConnell, D.D., in *The Churchman*, Jan. 23, 1897.

by others of their number who hate the term "Protestant." Leadership, too, in anything, it must be remembered, demands definiteness. Where that quality is so conspicuously wanting as here, what can one call all the talk of "a large, comprehensive, sympathetic view of the needs of American Christianity,"[1] as a plea for leadership, but well-meaning sentimentalism?

Many non-Catholic religious teachers are announcing "the return to Christ" as to mark the coming theology. What a confession or what a charge is veiled in such words! One of these men, whose "creed" made such a stir in their circles recently, says we are about through with the age of criticism, and are entering upon the age of mysticism again; that Christ is to be brought out "into the clear light of supreme belief"; that people are crying—"We don't care what men have said, what theologians are saying; let us have what Christ hath said."[2] With all our heart that is

[1] Rev. W. R. Huntington, D.D., at the Norfolk Church Congress, November, 1896. Dr. Huntington has more fully developed his ideas in his recent book, *A National Church*.
[2] Rev. John Watson, in *Boston Transcript*, Oct. 24, 1896.

what we wish might be,—*the return to Christ*. Not to some of His words, but to all of them; not merely to His ethical teachings about the Fatherhood of God and the brotherhood of men, which so many just now are making much of, which the Church has always held—West, too, as well as East, St. Augustine as well as Clement or Origen—but to what He taught about Himself, His Church and religion, the spiritual needs and destiny of men. Yes, let us have what Christ hath said. How many of His gracious words have been long despised or misinterpreted! There is no call to cite them. Men know them well enough, and how they have slighted them.

To speak in all seriousness, the return to Christ everywhere could mean, we believe, but one thing,—the triumph of the Catholic faith in the world. It could not be the setting up of the bald simplicity with which so many associate their thinking of Christ, which would do away with all idea of Church and dogma; it would be the acceptance of the one Church by Christ Himself established, with the teaching power of her doctrine, the dignity and glory of her worship, and the sway of both over the spiritual life. For this triumph of Christianity in the world the Holy Catholic Church unceasingly prays and strives. It is little for one or many to meet trial, discouragement, opposition, persecution. It is a joy to suffer and endure for the truth of God. Nothing else is to be compared. Nothing else is of importance. Everything is at stake. If the Catholic religion is not the religion of Christ, it is nothing; if it is that religion, it appeals to all who come within its reach with the exclusiveness of truth. Those who heed its appeal will find the sure remedy for the world's unrest.

Index

Anglicans, lost succession in breaking from the centre of unity, 70

Apostolicity, a decisive test of the true Church, 67; mistaken notions of, 67; relates to ministry, 69; the Pope necessary to, 70; relates to doctrine, 71, 72; true meaning of the apostolic spirit, 74–76

Antiquity, only part of the Church's claim, 76

Bishops, with the Pope at their head the Church's teaching power, 71; not mere deputies of the Holy See, 97

Boastfulness, too common among Catholics, 195

Calumny, how best met, 57

Catholic, as title of distinction from the sects, 60, 61; still a "prophetical" title, 64; religion, broadest in the world, 66, 196; Church in America, cannot be ignored, 225

Catholics, have hold upon great principles, 219; mainly responsible for transformation of Protestantism, 224; isolation of from Protestants, how far culpable, 224; power of religious life of, 225

Catholicity, meaning universality, 59; how the original idea was modified, 60; as related to unity, 64; as a finished quality, 65

Certainty and reality, the Catholic possession, 220; seen less and less in the Protestant world, 221

Choice, responsibility of, with the inquirer, 212

Christ, the return to, would mean the triumph of the Catholic faith, 228, 229

Christianity, implies the Church, 13

Church, no, no Christianity, 13; vague notions of the, among Protestants, 14, etc.; as only invisible, a despairing idea, 24; both visible and invisible, 23, 26; soul and body of the, 27; unchangeable, yet adapting herself, 33; growth of the, 63, 138, 202; notes of the, to be taken together, 64; visible headship of in the Pope, revealing the heavenly headship in Christ, 93; a monarchy, yet governed by the bishops, sharing the Pope's authority, 97; government of, not a tyranny, 98; see also "Unity," "Holiness," "Catholicity," "Apostolicity."

Circumstances, power of, with inquirers, 202

Clergy, holy lives of the, 187

Communion, frequency of, 109

Compromise *vs.* Comprehensiveness, 17

Confession, as a prerequisite of Communion, 111; to a priest, why necessary, 141; to God, also taught, 142; moderate requirements in, 146; abuses in connection with, 147; yet the confessional a bulwark of all right living, 148; Protestant world worse off without it, 148

Conscience, no one's in hands of the priest, 146

Contrition, perfect, implying confession to a priest when possible, 142

Definiteness, of the Church's teaching, springing from her divine authority, 34

Index

Definitions, new, do not mean new revelations, 41, 84
Development, of dogma of Papal Infallibility, 83, 85 ; of the Immaculate Conception, 129 ; a genuine development consistent with fixed revelation, 223, *and references*.
Devotion, see " Virgin," and " Saints."

Episcopalians, vagueness of their ideas of the Church, 17
Eucharist, Real Presence of Christ in the, 101 ; Zwinglian, Lutheran, and Anglican substitutes for this teaching, 102, etc. ; means His entire presence, 105 ; the only reasonable interpretation of Christ's words, 106 ; no denial of evidence of the senses, 106 ; adoration of the, 108 ; why given in only one kind to the people, 109

Faith, a reasonable, required, 32 ; *vs.* opinion, 33 ; unity of, 40, 46 ; given its true place by the doctrine of merit, 160
Free-thought, its beginning and its consequences, 122

Heathen, the, not left without hope, 29
Heretics, *bona-fide*, morally members of the visible Church, 29
Holiness, a necessary attribute of the Church, 49 ; degrees of among her members, 52 ; not naturally demonstrative, 50 ; various types of, 52 ; among the poor, 51 ; progress towards the ideal of, 53 ; genuine, found outside the visible Church, 54
Human sympathy, the saints appeal to, 174

Images, veneration of, explained, 182
Indefectible, the Church, because apostolic, 73

Indulgences, what they are, 154; benefit of, 154; their abuse, 155; why misunderstood and misrepresented, 156

Infallibility, of the Church, 72; of the Pope, 83, etc.; see "Pope."

Inquirers, honest, must conquer circumstances, 206; and conquer themselves, 208; what constitutes an inquirer, 207; must use reason and act upon it, 208, 210; must submit their will, 211; various motives of, 211

Investigation, of Catholic claims should be honest and thorough, 209

Jealousies, among Catholics of different races, 198

Journalism, Catholic, improvement needed in, 193

Latin, as the language of the Mass, 119

Lenity, a wise, not to be called laxity, 110

Liberal, A Catholic who is truly, not to be condemned, 196

Liberalism, to be condemned, 196; aggressiveness of in our time, 221

Liberty, of worship in the Mass, 45; of devotions, see "Virgin," and "Saints."

Light, danger of sinning against, 212

Liturgies, the Eastern, strong teaching of, concerning the Blessed Virgin, 129

Love, for Jesus can still keep in mind His promised reward, 167; might be more manifested among Catholics, 197

Luther, originating the idea of the invisible Church, 24; ground for his theory of consubstantiation, 103; his attack upon indulgences, 155; his false notions of faith and merit, 158; his false teaching concerning sin, 137, 159

Index

Mass, the, teaching unity of worship, 44; the highest act of worship, 112; a true sacrifice, 113; mystical, 114; essentially one with the Sacrifice on the Cross, 115; available for the dead, 115, etc.; in memory of saints, 117; the people offering, with the priest, 118; Latin as the language of, 119; reasonableness of all Catholic teaching concerning, 114, 118, 121; too rapid saying of, deprecated, 190; possible explanations, 191; evils of the practice, 192, 193

Merit, the idea reasonable and necessary, 157; first strenuously opposed by Luther, 157; still shocking to the orthodox Protestant, 158; a corollary to the Catholic doctrine of justification, 158; gives faith its true place, but makes action also necessary, 160; Bible full of Catholic teaching of, 161; does not encourage self-righteousness, 162; our merits, God's gifts, 162; may be lost and regained, 163; degrees of, 163; this life the only time for gaining, 164; power of as a motive, compared with suffering, 165; how the Church's prayers teach, 166; what the motive accomplishes in life, 166, 167; gaining reward of heaven not a mercenary matter, 167; as the ground of appeal to the world's unrest, 168

Miracles, now as well as in first age of the Church, 173

Natural religion, as the foundation of supernatural, 10; can not meet man's needs and aspirations, 10; made our only hope by modern liberalism, 222

Obstacles, Catholics presenting great personal, to the acceptance of their religion, 184, etc.; exist in inquirers themselves, 201, etc.

Occupation and pecuniary support, question of, as a hindrance to inquirers, 203

Optimism, a false, in relation to sin, 137

Penance, the sacrament of, 140 ; the ancient and the modern, 151

Perfunctoriness, of many clergymen, 190

Persecution, possible, of those who become Catholics, 205

Peter, St., grants made to, explained, 70, 82, 94

Pope, primacy of the, not merely honorary, but one of jurisdiction, 82 ; a gradual development, 83 ; reasonableness of, 82, 91 ; what it has accomplished, 94 ; infallibility of the, follows from his primacy, 83 ; though recently defined, not a novelty, 84 ; consistently developed, 85 ; limitations of the Vatican definition, 86, 88 ; pertains only to his office, and in definite exercise, 90 ; reasonableness of, 91, 95 ; its difficulties not made light of, but the doctrine held with moderation, 96

Prayer, as a means, with inquirers, 212

Preaching, need of improvement in, 188

Prejudice, against the Catholic religion still active, 79 ; how to be treated, 80 ; persistent concerning devotion to the Blessed Virgin, and other saints, 124, 178

Priesthood of the faithful, recognized, 119

Protestantism, vagueness concerning the Church, inherent in, 16 ; not yet dead, 196 ; uncertainty and unreality of, 221 ; perhaps becoming Catholicized, 223 ; leadership of, only a sentimentalism, 227

Punishment eternal, Catholic teaching concerning, 149 ; how different from that of Calvinism, 150 ; temporal, scope of the idea, 151

Index

Purgatory, little taught concerning, 150; doctrine of, reasonable, 153; not for future probation, 164

Real Presence, the central truth of the Eucharist, 120; its denial leads to all free-thought, 121
Reason, inquirers must use and act upon, 208, 210
Reasonableness, of Catholic teaching in general, 32; as to Papal infallibility, 35, 95; as to the Eucharist, 105; as to the Mass, 114, 118; as to the Blessed Virgin, 125, etc.; as to sin and confession, 141, 145; as to punishment, 150; as to purgatory and indulgences, 153, 154; as to merit, 157; as to the Saints, 176, 180, 182
Relics, veneration of explained, 181
Reward, eternal, according to merit, 163; but not a mercenary matter, 167

Sacraments, the, unfailing bonds of unity, 44
Sacrifice, the Mass a true, 113
Saints, known and unknown, 54; wide meaning of the word, 170; how understood by the Church, 170; varied character and gifts among the, 171; not always our examples, 171; but always in sanctity, 172; as mirrors of Christ, 172; unjust criticism of their lives, 173; the communion of, appeals to human sympathy, 174; science of the, a source of strength, 175; intercede for us, 176; we may ask their help, 177; their mediatorship does not take honor from Christ, 178; veneration of, essentially differs from worship paid to God, 180; and a safeguard against revival of idolatry, 181; relics and images of the, why venerated, and objections answered, 181, 182
Satisfaction, the principle of, 151

Secular, spiritualizing of the, in Catholic life, 225

Sin, Christianity presupposes, 136 ; the fact evident, and increasing cause of the world's unrest, 137-139 ; disastrous results of false teaching concerning, 138 ; the Church teaches its dread reality, and pardon only through Christ's merits, 139, 140 ; these merits applied in sacraments, 140 ; particularly in Penance, 140 ; a tribunal in this sacrament, 141 ; and the sinner his own accuser, 141 ; confession of to the priest, need of and objections answered, 141-143 ; the secrets of, kept, 144 ; grievous, or mortal, and venial, a wise distinction, 145 ; Protestantism makes too much or too little of, 145, 149 ; as to punishment of, the Church's teaching reasonable, 149 ; satisfaction for, 151 ; purgatory, the place of temporal punishment of, 152

Social position, loss of by those who become Catholics, 204

Suffering, Catholic teaching dignifies, 151 ; see also " Merit."

Tact, needed in matters of religion, 206

Truth, *vs.* " truths," in religion, 64, 222

Unholiness, in the visible Church, 56

Unity, of the Church, spiritual and organic, 38 ; of faith, 40 ; of government, 42 ; of worship and sacraments, 44, 45 ; a centre of, the leading idea of her government, 42 ; not lost, 46 ; wanderers are to return to, 47 ; how injured by lack of love, 197

Unrest, its source, 1 ; present causes, 2 ; manifestations, 3 ; purpose, 4 ; its remedy, in Christ's religion, 5 ; unity as bearing upon, 45 ; as related to Catholicity, 66 ; as related to apostolicity, 68 ; truth of the Real Presence bearing upon, 121, 122 ; devotion to the Blessed Virgin helping to free the

Index

world from, 131, 134 ; from sin, increasing, 137, 139, 149 ; worth of the motive of *merit*, in appealing to, 168 ; the Catholic religion finds field for men's restless powers, 168 ; could be helped by acceptance of Catholic truth about the Saints, 176 ; various aspects of, 214, 215 ; marking all civilization, and on the increase, 216 ; remedy for, as wide-reaching as the need, and in the Catholic religion, 217 ; cessation of can be only gradual, 218, 219 ; and reaching perfection only in the future life, 220 ; admitted by Protestants, 20, 226

Virgin, the Blessed, highest of creatures, 123 ; Catholic belief in and devotion to, natural, 123 ; the Mother of God, 125 ; preserved from original sin, 126 ; redeemed by Christ, 126 ; her sinless life, 128 ; dogma of her Immaculate Conception, 129, etc.; the definition guards the truth of the Incarnation, 130 ; fitness of devotion to, 131 ; it strengthens loyalty to Jesus Christ, 132 ; "impassable distance" between her and Him, 132 ; liberty of devotion to, 133 ; what her intercession means, 133 ; ; appeals to reverence and affection, 134 ; knows the world's unrest, 134 ; the model for Christian women, 135

Will, submission of the, necessary, 211; God will not coerce the, 212

www.ingramcontent.com/pod-product-compliance
Lightning Source LLC
Chambersburg PA
CBHW031737230426
43669CB00007B/372